Vital Signs of Christ's Return

The 77 Most-Asked Questions on Christ's Return!

Vital Signs
of
Christ's
Return

The 77 Most-Asked Questions on Christ's Return!

Ray W. Yerbury

New Leaf Press

New Leaf Press Edition
June 1995

ISBN: 0-89221-293-4
Library of Congress: 95-69890

Unless otherwise noted, all Scripture references are from the
New International Version, ©1984, International Bible
Society. Used by permission of Zondervan Bible Publish-
ers.

Acknowledgment

My very good friend, Dr. Clifford Wilson, president emeritus of Pacific College of Graduate Studies, Melbourne, Australia, and others have painstakingly proofread this manuscript and offered numerous helpful suggestions which were incorporated into the final product. For this I am indeed most grateful.

Dedication

This book is dedicated to my family:
Lynette, my loving wife and very best friend,
Jeffrey and his wife Toni, and Mark — my two sons.

Contents

Foreword 9

Preface 13

1. The Prophets 19
2. General Questions 25
3. The Jewish Nation 35
4. The Church Age 57
5. Satan, the Antichrist, the False Prophet 73
6. The Tribulation Judgments 83
7. The Second Coming of Jesus Christ 101
8. The Millennial Kingdom 109
9. The Eternal Kingdom 129
10. Current Prophetic Issues 139

Charts

1. Prophets of Israel and Judah 23
2. Future for Planet Earth 32
3. Israel: Sequence of World Events 33
4. Tribulation Judgment 43
5. End of this Age: Beginning of a New Era 54
6. Millennial & Tribulation Views 66
7. Church Age to Eternal State 72
8. Activity during the Tribulation 91
9. The Second Coming of Jesus Christ 107
10. The World's Last Three Battles 137

Tables

1. Important Historical Dates 47

2. Contrast between Christ and Antichrist 81

3. Characteristics and Nature of the Millennium 122

Diagrams

1. Sheol — Hades 31

2. The Star of David 44

3. The Greenhouse Effect 163

Maps

1. Israel & Judah in Exile 15

2. The Land of Gog & Magog 16

3. The Promised Land 17

Foreword

Ray Yerbury's book, *Vital Signs of Christ's Return*, represents an attempt to answer popular questions asked by rank and file members of present-day churches. There is no doubt that many inside and outside the Church are greatly concerned with the possible end of our civilization's development toward overpopulation, deforestation, rampant pollution — and above all, a seeming inevitable nuclear holocaust.

To understand what the Bible has to say about these possibilities in relation to God's plan for our planet and its people requires interpretations at three different levels:

First there are the clearly defined aspects such as the return of Christ to the earth in splendor and world dominion, and the resurrection of the saints in association with Him. The author of *Vital Signs* has allowed the natural understanding of the Scriptures to determine the important points in the "plan of the ages."

Secondly, we have attempts to explain many relevant passages in line with the commentator's understanding (or bias) of the overall picture of coming events, and their divine purpose and outcome. In this area the problems of the relation of the Old Testament to the New Testament, of the Church to Israel, and a definition of the "kingdom of God" often determine (and sometimes cloud) the understanding of Holy Writ. Humbleness of attitude is required so that we let the Scriptures speak for themselves rather than a preconceived acceptance of a "scheme of interpretation" established by a prior reasoning.

Ray Yerbury attempts to answer these questions in the light of the overall plan he perceives in the total biblical picture. The general outline is not distorted.

He accepts realistically the blueprint of God's plan revealed by Him in the unalterable Abrahamic covenant oath (Gen. 12:1-3, 22:16-18; Acts 3:25-26; Gal. 3:13-14; Heb. 6:13-20).

This involves a recognition that God has permanent plans for the great nation of Israel as well as global salvation purposes for the nations of the world. These salvation purposes include, but do not exhaust, the production and destiny of the Church in its special relation to Christ as His bride — an aspect in God's overall plan which was hidden in the Old Testament but revealed to the Apostles (Eph. 3:3-7; Col. 1:24-27). All the drama of final world events will reveal God's divine intention has always been that everything revolves around the one person, Jesus Christ (Eph. 1:9-10). Christ must fulfill human history before any final consummation can occur beyond history (1 Cor. 15:24-28).

God created a world environment and put man in it to manage it for his Creator (Gen. 1:26-28). Even man's first failure did not cancel this program of God (Ps. 8:3-8), as Hebrews 2:6-9 clearly indicates. It is completely fulfilled by a reigning Christ in and over the world, which God made to be inhabited and not destroyed (Isa. 45:18). In all the cardinal aspects of this overall plan it seems to me that Ray is faithful to Scripture.

There is thirdly and characteristically, an attempt to explain the scriptural texts in the light of present-day happenings, which, however, so frequently are found to be passé. To prognosticate is to be human. One of God's purposes in revealing future events related to divine goals is that we might understand the days in which we live, but not necessarily the days of all the many tomorrows. Yet we must prognosticate, but always tentatively and within the framework of the scripturally obvious and the final revealed goals. Ray has some very readable material in his prognostications.

One can follow Ray's overall scheme with profit, though at a number of points I would have given different answers to the questions asked.

Dr. E. Gibson, M.A., B.Ed., B.Sc.(Econ.)., B.D., Th.D.

Preface

We are living far nearer to the time of Christ's return than most people would care to realize. I am positive of this fact from two points of view:

1. The many clear signs now evident in the world that Jesus spoke about in His Olivet Discourse recorded in Matthew 24 and 25. In particular, the gathering storm clouds surrounding the nation of Israel are highly relevant.

2. The great increase in interest among individual Christians of things pertaining to the return of our Lord Jesus Christ with power and great glory.

It is abundantly clear that the Church worldwide is keeping strangely quiet about anything remotely connected to the Second Advent. There is hardly a trumpet being sounded from the pulpits to warn the people of the fast approach of that great and wonderful "day of the Lord." In fact, many of our spiritual leaders are like ostriches with their heads buried in the sand, while their congregations are in a state of semi-animation.

As I travel throughout Australia and overseas, I meet Christians from all walks of life and religious persuasions. What fascinates me most is that I am constantly bombarded with questions about end-time events. There is a thirst for the truth as revealed in Scripture. However, there is also much confusion in this area of Second Coming teaching, and that's exactly the situation Satan would want.

Many of the questions contained in this book are being asked continually by both Christians and non-Christians attending Second Coming conferences, weekend seminars, and church and home fellowship meetings.

Naturally, there are many additional questions about Christ's return that might have been included. However, I have endeavored to confine the list of 77 questions to the most frequently asked and the most relevant and helpful for today's living. In providing answers to these questions I have been conscious of the leading of the Holy Spirit who provides the wisdom of understanding for all Scripture. Furthermore, I have been acutely aware and careful not to attach my own fanciful ideas as to what I would like to see take place in the end-time drama.

The plain straight-forward Word of God should never be fitted into man-made systems that depend more on mental ingenuity than on sound exegesis. Only the actual events of our Lord's first coming threw light on Moses and the prophets. Consequently, many of our blueprints for the future might well be found to be out-of-scale as we see events unfold before our eyes.

It is my prayer that each reader will seek wisdom and clear understanding from the Holy Spirit as he or she continues to search the Scriptures for a "more sure word of prophecy" (2 Pet. 1:19;KJV). This is important, but a prayerful interest in taking the gospel to the lost in a godless materialistic and degenerate world is equally important and very urgent.

— Ray Yerbury

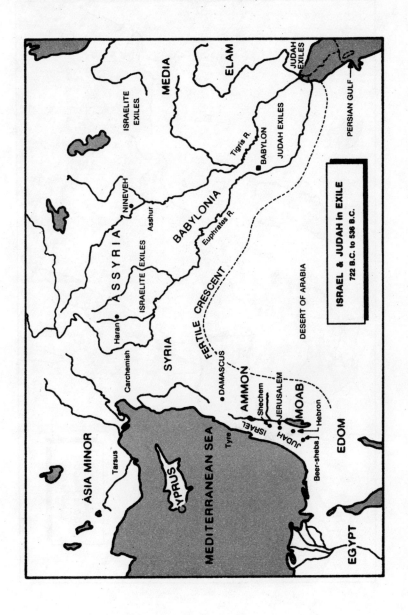

Map 1 — Israel & Judah in Exile

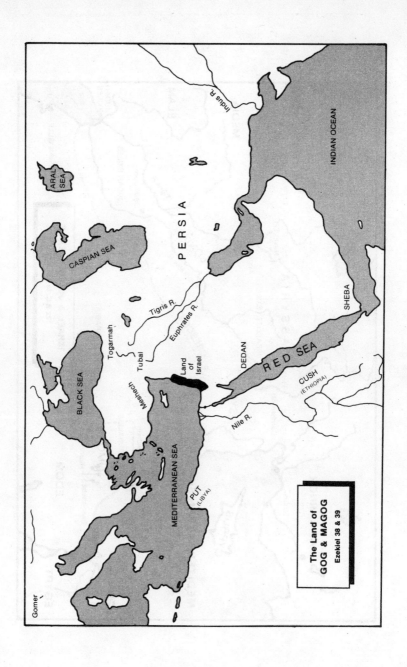

Map 2 — The Land of Gog & Magog

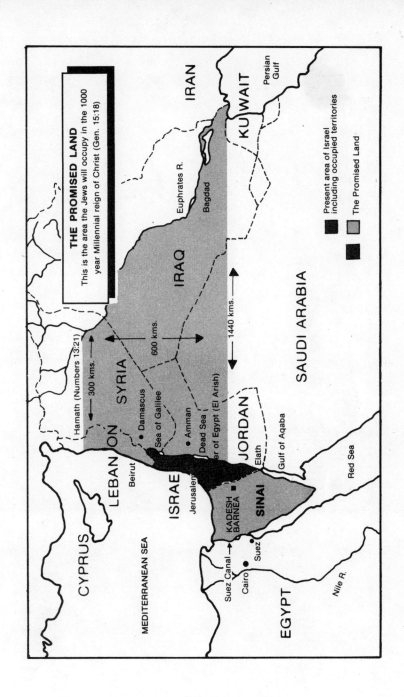

Map 3 — The Promised Land

1
The Prophets

1. Question: Are there any prophets in the world today?

Answer: The Bible gives very clear reference to the fact that we are to beware of false prophets (Matt. 7:15; Mark 13:22; 2 Pet. 2:1).

In Matthew 24, which together with 25 is called the "Olivet Discourse," Jesus says, "Many false prophets will appear and deceive many people" (Matt. 24:11). Jesus was referring to that period of time I believe we are living in today. He was giving one of the signs of the *end of the age.*

The last biblical prophet was John, the son of Zebedee, one of the 12 apostles. He wrote the Book of Revelation, the last great apocalyptic writing in the canon of Scripture.

No! There are no prophets in the world today such as there were in the Old Testament period and the first century A.D. The gift of prophecy given to the New Testament church as detailed in Ephesians 4:11, is not one of foretelling, but rather of forthtelling the clear message of Christ's imminent return recorded in Holy Scripture from as early as the prophet Enoch.

This prophecy of Enoch is recorded in Jude 14. He quotes from a first-century pseudepigraphal book, *The Book of Enoch.* In doing so he is not affirming the authority of this book, but rather using it to illustrate a point, much as Paul did when he cited the Greek poets Aratus (Acts 17:28) and Epimenides (Titus 1:12).

Never before in history have there been so many self-proclaimed prophets as we have today. They are people of borrowed testimony in a self-appointed ministry, directing their energies toward predicting dates for Christ's return.

But we are not privy to when prophesied events will happen, or even their exact sequence. What is most important is not that we know the prophetic timetable as such, but that we understand how to live while we are waiting for Jesus to return. However, we can know the signs, we can watch, and we can learn the lessons (Matt. 24).

2. Question: What do we mean by the phrase: "Prophecy's First Word"?

Answer: The first word of prophecy recorded in the Bible is found in Genesis 3:15. It is known as the "Proto-Evangel," the first gospel, or the "Edenic Covenant."

It is a conversation between God and Satan where God predicts Satan will be defeated at the Cross and finally destroyed in the "Lake of Fire" as detailed in Revelation 20:10. What this particular verse is saying in simple language is this: God says to Satan, "I've got news for you Satan. You think that you have won the 'Battle of Eden' but you haven't. You might bruise the heel of my Son, but in the process He will crush your head."[1]

We know from science that a snake has no antibodies to fight an open wound. Hence, when a snake is injured, particularly if it is crushed, the inevitable result is death to the snake. On the other hand, it is highly unlikely that anyone would die from the bruised heel.

Prophecy's first word from man regarding the second coming of Christ is found in Jude 14: "Enoch, the seventh from Adam, prophesied about these men: 'See, the Lord is coming with thousands upon thousands of his holy ones.' "

3. Question: Who is considered to be the greatest prophet?

Answer: The man of God that immediately comes to mind is Moses. He was quite a remarkable person. Apart from Jesus Christ, Moses was the only man in Jewish history who exercised the office of prophet (Deut. 34:10), priest (Num. 12:7), and king.[2] Moses was never made king, but he functioned as the ruler of Israel.

During the inter-testamental period, no prophet arose for 400 years. The next great prophetic utterance was delivered by John the Baptist, announcing the coming of Jesus Christ (John 1:15). It was Jesus who said, "I tell you the truth: Among those born of women there has not risen anyone greater than John the Baptist" (Matt. 11:11).

Summarizing: Jesus was basically saying that John the Baptist was as great as any prophet. To answer the question, however, Moses would certainly head the long list of great prophets. God said that he was the most humble man on the face of the earth (Num. 12:3), and without question he achieved more in his lifetime than any other man in history (apart from the Lord, of course).

4. Question: Which minor prophet predicted events covering the greatest time expanse in history?

Answer: The prophet Micah. He prophesied to both Israel and Judah around 725 B.C. He was a contemporary of Isaiah. Micah shows God's hatred of His people's passionless ritual and sin, and offers pardon to them. Judgment will be followed by restoration and forgiveness. The book with the same name as the man, Micah, ends on a strong note of promise. Micah's predictions were:

1. Israel's captivity by Assyria in 722 B.C. (Mic. 1: 6).

2. Judah's captivity by Babylon in 586 B.C. (Mic. 4:10).

3. The birthplace of the Messiah (Mic. 5:2).

4. The trial of Christ (Mic. 5:1 — compare with Matt. 27:30).

5. Destruction of Jerusalem and the temple in A.D. 70 (Mic. 3:12).

6. The millennial reign of Christ on this earth (Mic. 4:1).

It should be noted that the "princely prophet" Isaiah stands tall above all the prophets of the Old Testament in terms of the number of separate predictions. Furthermore, they extended in time beyond Micah's to include the eternal reign of the Father (Isa. 65:17).

5. Question: What is the difference between forthtelling and foretelling?

Answer: The prophets of the Old Testament as well as John the Baptist (the linchpin prophet, who through his ministry makes the transition from law to grace) were primarily forthtellers — addressing messages to the people of their generation.

In addition, some of them were also foretellers — telling forth God's will and purpose, of events to take place well into the future. They were foretellers because their day was only a moment in the progress of a divine plan. The beloved apostle John would be considered a *foreteller*.

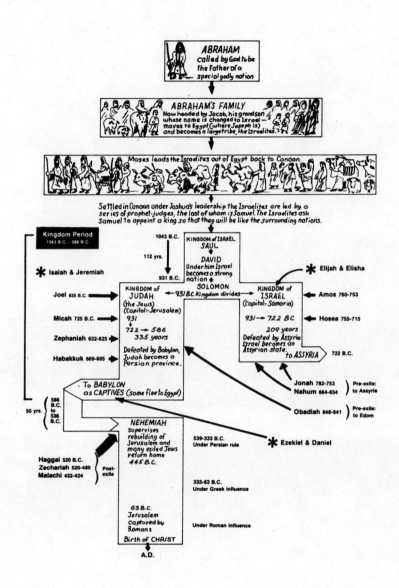

Chart 1. Prophets of Israel and Judah

2
General Questions

6. Question: Isn't there some doubt in people's minds that Christ will ever return? Doesn't His delay contribute to this doubt?

Answer: The apostle Peter said: "You must understand that in the last days scoffers will come, scoffing and following their own evil desires. They will say, 'Where is this "coming" he promised? Ever since our fathers died, everything goes on as it has since the beginning of creation' " (2 Pet. 3:3-4).

It is interesting to note that these people are not just intellectual scoffers. They are people who know something about the Scriptures. But because of their own evil desires and sin, they rationalize away the clear teachings of the Word of God.

The people in Noah's day did not believe that a flood was coming, but it did. And similarly today, multitudes do not believe judgment is coming, BUT IT WILL!

Now, to answer the question we must reach back into the Old Testament. In Genesis 5:21 we read of Methuselah — the eighth in generation line from Adam. He was the grandfather of Noah and an ancestor of Christ, and the longest living human recorded in the Bible.

According to Fausset's *Bible Encyclopedia,* his name means "He dies and it is sent." What is it that is sent? Seven days after Methuselah died, the worldwide biblical flood began.[3]

What is the message from Scripture? God gave man the maximum life span to repent before the Flood. This was approximately 1,000 years. He is doing exactly the same today in the Church era, except the life span has been reduced to 120 years (Gen. 6:3).

In 2 Peter 3:9 we read: "The Lord is not slow in keeping his promise, as some understand slowness. He is patient with you, not wanting anyone to perish, but everyone to come to repentance."

7. Question: How can we prove that the Bible is in fact God's inspired Word?

Answer: William Gladstone, the English statesman, once declared that the Bible is "The impregnable rock." How true that statement is. It is indeed the revelation of God to man, the only Book that will lead man to God. Why? Because —

1. It is the inspired Word of God (2 Tim. 3:16; 2 Pet. 1:21).
2. It is infallible (Ps. 19:7).
3. It is inerrant (Prov. 30:5-6).
4. It is complete (Rev. 22:18-19).
5. It is authoritative (John 20:31).
6. It is sufficient (2 Tim. 3:15).
7. It is the source of truth (John 17:17).
8. It is the source of happiness (Prov. 30:5-6; Luke 11:28).
9. It is the source of power (Heb. 4:12).
10. It is the source of guidance (Ps. 19:7-8).
11. It is comfort (Rom. 15:4).
12. It is the source of victory (Eph. 6:17).

The Bible is the inspired Word of God:

1. Because of the claims of Scripture. The phrase "Thus

said the Lord" and other similar expressions occur over 2,000 times in the Old Testament alone.

Paul declared, "All Scripture is God-breathed and is useful for teaching, rebuking, correcting and training in righteousness, so that the man of God may be thoroughly equipped for every good work" (2 Tim. 3:16-17).

Other references include 2 Peter 1:21 and Hebrews 1:1.

2. *Because of the Harmony of Scripture.* No man is capable of bringing together, without error, 66 books written by over 40 different earthly scribes in 15 different generations, composed upon three different continents, surrounded by different environments, using kings, priests, a doctor, shepherds, fishermen, a prime minister, and a tax collector. Only God can do that, with a continuity, oneness, and accord that declares God alone is the author.

3. *Because of the manuscripts of Scripture.* The findings in Assyrian palaces have vindicated the factuality of many people mentioned in the Old Testament portion of Scripture.

The Dead Sea Scrolls date by 1,000 years all previously discovered scripts in Hebrew, and authenticate the prophecy of Isaiah.

4. *Archaeological confirmation of Scripture.* Archaeology has:

a. Demonstrated the accuracy of biblical customs. Rachel stole her father's clay gods (Gen. 31:32) because they were a form of title deed.

b. Used appropriate language in different cultural settings — e.g. Joseph, overseer in Egypt (Gen. 41:40); and added information to Bible words — as with the Assyrian battles.

c. Confirmed specific incidents as with Isaiah 20:1 concerning the Assyrian attack against the Philistine city of Ashdod.

5. *Because of fulfilled prophecies of Scripture.* Most of the fulfilled prophecies relate to Christ — His birth, death,

resurrection, and Second Coming (Gen. 3:15; Ps. 16:10; Mic. 5:2; Isa. 7, 9, 11, 53, 61).

Others relate to Israel (Jer. 16:14-16; Ezek. 37:12-14); the outpouring of the Holy Spirit (Acts 2); and the prediction about world conditions prior to the Second Coming (Dan. 12:4; Matt. 24).

Only God our Creator can write history in advance with total perfect accuracy.

8. Question: Many people say that the study of prophecy is irrelevant and unprofitable — Jesus will come only when He's good and ready! What is the biblical response to such a question?

Answer: The Bible clearly reveals that a knowledge of prophecy is spiritually stimulating. After all, one-third of the Bible is devoted to prophecy, and heeding the prophetic Word will give the believer the clearest instruction regarding our present walk and ultimate destination in life.

We must also understand that our faith is based on all of God's Word, not just a particular section or favorite verses and passages.

Our spiritual walk should always be a careful balance between *working, waiting,* and *watching.* Through waiting and watching, we will learn to know Him more intimately which will result in our being increasingly transformed into His image. The Bible says, "When he appears, we shall be like him, for we shall see him as he is" (1 John 3:2).

The Lord not only exhorts us to "watch," but this watchfulness is expressed in the requirements of highest activity for the believer — prayer! (Luke 12:36).

I believe a recognition of His imminent return must lead to a deeper fellowship and closeness to Christ. This intimate relationship will require purification. "Everyone who has this hope in him purifies himself, just as he is pure" (1 John 3:3).

9. Question: How long is a generation?

Answer: When Jesus was speaking to His disciples on the Mount of Olives just prior to His crucifixion, He said among many things concerning the "end times," in what has become known as the "Olivet Discourse," "This generation will certainly not pass away until all these things have happened" (Matt. 24:34).

What things? All the judgments as outlined in the preceding verses in Matthew 24, referring to events during the disciples' liftime, together with those that must occur during the Tribulation in the end times.

What Jesus was referring to in this statement was the "fig tree," considered by many scholars as the symbol of the nation of Israel — i.e., Israel as a self-governing nation in its own land. For over 2,500 years, since the final captivity to Babylon by Nebuchadnezzar in 586 B.C., and the re-establishment of Israel as a nation in 1948, Israel has been a persecuted and scattered people.

It must also be noted that Dr. Luke refers not only to the "fig-tree," but "all the trees." This is a reference to all the nations that come upon Israel in the final days leading to the campaign of Armageddon.

I believe there are five possible definitions of "a generation."

1. A period of 40 years, the duration of the wilderness wanderings (Num. 32:13).

2. Psalm 90:10 acquaints us with the general length of a generation as 70 or 80 years.

3. Four "generations" of Abraham's descendants occupied a time span of 400 years — 100 years for a generation (Gen. 15:13).

4. A "generation" could extend from the birth of the longest living person born after the time commenced, until that person died — perhaps 120 years.

5. Sometimes 25 years is put forward as being about the average time for becoming a parent.

10. Question: The Bible speaks about hell, hades, and sheol. What is their relationship?

Answer: Hell is generally used in the Old Testament to translate the Hebrew word sheol. It simply means the place of the dead without reference to happiness (Gen. 37:35, 42:38; 1 Sam. 2:6; Job 14:13). In other passages the idea of punishment is conveyed.

The Authorized Version (AV) and the King James Version (KJV) both use the word "grave" instead of sheol. The Revised Standard Version (RSV) retains the Hebrew word.

In the New Testament the word hell (KJV; AV) is used to translate two words: (1) Hades: the place of the dead; and, (2) Gehenna: the place of retribution for evil deeds. This word is derived from *ge-hinnom*, and means the valley of the sons of Hinnom. It was an actual place — the valley that enclosed Jerusalem from the west and south; where children were sacrificed to the god Molech (2 Kings 23:10); and the location of the Jerusalem rubbish dump.

Hades (RSV) generally means the same as sheol, the region of departed spirits of the lost, but includes the blessed dead in periods preceding the resurrection of Christ. Paradise was the upper compartment of hades (Luke 23:43).

Sheol is derived from a word meaning "the deep place." This word is used in the Old Testament for the place of the dead.

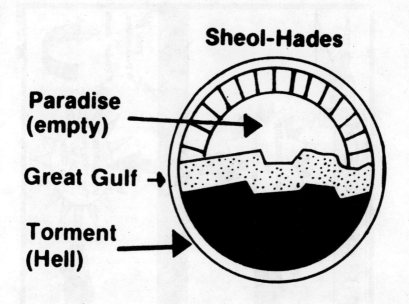

Diagram 1. Sheol/Hades

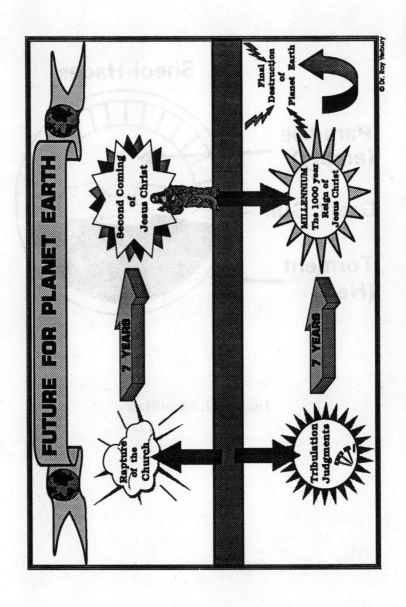

Chart 2. Future For Planet Earth

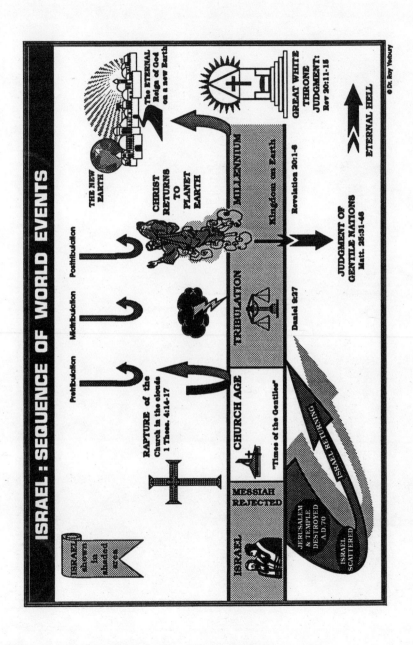

Chart 3. Sequence of World Events

3
The Jewish Nation

11. Question: Why was the nation of Israel chosen by God as a special identity?

Answer: Although the Jews look to Abraham as their father, strictly speaking they are descendants of Jacob, whose name was changed to Israel by Jehovah (Gen. 32:28)

Note: Not all Abraham's descendants were Jews. His other son Ishmael became the forefather of the Arab races. Similarly, not all those who sprung from Isaac were Jews either. Esau became the father of the Edomites, who were to become a thorn in the side of Israel for centuries, and this is still valid today.

To ask why God chose such a people is to ask a question to which there is no answer. It is beyond all human understanding. Israel's election is an outstanding evidence of the sovereign grace of God.

Apart from Abraham's clear-cut faith as shown in Hebrews 11:8-10, there was certainly no outstanding reason why God should choose the Israelites and not some other race. But then, there was no compelling reason why God should have chosen me for salvation. The answer lies exclusively in the sovereign grace of God.

12. Question: How did the first coming of Christ affect the history of Israel?

Answer: According to the New Testament, Jesus Christ is a true son of Israel. This is distinctly recorded in the first verse of Matthew chapter 1: "A record of the genealogy of Jesus Christ the son of David, the son of Abraham."

Jesus, born of the Virgin Mary, was the Messiah whom God had sent to reconcile all men, both Jews and pagans, to himself (Acts 2:36; 2 Cor. 5:19). In other words God, who spoke to His people through the prophets in times past, now chose to speak to all people by His Son.

The promise made to Abraham of the seed in whom all the families of the earth would be blessed, had been fulfilled in Christ.

The coming of Jesus Christ established forever the forgiveness of sins, not by animal sacrifice, but through Christ who shed His blood on Calvary. That is the heart of the gospel. The peace with God through Christ effectively broke down the barriers between Jew and Gentile (Eph. 2:14-22). Unfortunately, perfect union between Jew and Gentile will only be realized at the time of the Marriage Supper of the Lamb (Rev. 19:7-9).

Today we live in the period of history known as the time of the Gentiles, a time when Jesus Christ is building His Church. For the Jew it is a time of partial rejection. Eventually the nation of Israel (or a remnant of the nation) will be saved (Rom. 11:25-26).

13. Question: Is the modern state of Israel a fulfillment of prophecy? Is there a future for Israel?

Answer: In Matthew 16:1-4 we read that our Lord rebuked the people of His day because they failed to recognize the significance of the times. They could read the signs of the weather but not national spiritual trends. Their eyes were blinded to observing the meaning of contemporary history. This condition is not unlike our present generation who is totally preoccupied with worldly circumstances.

Under the divine judgment of God, the Jews were torn away from their land just over 2,500 years ago in 586 B.C. A minority returned to Jerusalem from captivity in Babylon commencing 50 years later, but it was to a land under Gentile rule. All this was to no avail because in A.D. 70 the temple and the city of Jerusalem was totally destroyed as prophesied by Jesus (Matt. 24:2). From the captivity until today the majority of the Jews have been a landless, persecuted, scattered people.

In spite of all this they have never lost their identity, and we now see in our generation the re-establishment of Israel in the Promised Land. Although the Jew is returning largely in unbelief, there is nothing in history quite so remarkable.

God is not finished with the Jew. Liberal scholars typically ignore any reference to Israel. Even some within the ranks of conservative evangelicalism state quite openly that God is finished with Israel, and that the Jew has been set aside and superseded by the Church composed of Jews and Gentiles.

What do the critics say?

There are many aspects taken totally out of context. One such approach comes from the words of Jesus who declared, "Believe me, woman, a time is coming when you will worship the Father neither on this mountain nor in Jerusalem" (John 4:21).

Critics say that Jerusalem in Palestine was abolished forever as to its spiritual significance. They further argue that the Zion referred to in Isaiah 59:20-21, and Romans 11:26-27 can only refer to the New Testament Zion, i.e., the Church of our Saviour, Jesus Christ!

To argue in this manner betokens a failure to differentiate between Israel and the Church. They cannot in any way be united into one identity. They must be distinguished as two separate entities with whom God is dealing in a parallel program. However, one day, at the time of Christ's second coming, we will see a beautiful union of Jewish and Gentile saints. Then finally, God's hidden treasure — the nation of Israel, and His precious pearl — a glorified Church, will shine together in those nail-scarred hands which redeemed both Israel and the Church on Calvary's hill (Matt. 13:44-50).

It is foolish to attempt to interpret certain Old and New Testament prophecies relative to Israel otherwise than literally, and the idea of spiritualizing such prophecies and applying them to the Church is to go against the clear teachings of Scripture and common sense.

14. Question: What did Paul mean when he said, "All Israel will be saved"?

Answer: To say that Israel is finished and there is no future for the nation is to come perilously close to saying that God is not true to His covenants, and is therefore a liar.

Scripture presents Israel's possession of the land as being the unbreakable covenant of God: " 'To your descendants I give this land, from the river of Egypt to the great river, the Euphrates' " (Gen. 15:18).

When the Lord brought Israel out of bondage into Canaan it was because He ". . . remembered his covenant with Abraham, with Isaac and with Jacob" (Exod. 2:24). It was an unconditional promise, made by the Lord in full knowledge of what Israel's behavior would be. It was a sovereign purpose from which it is impossible that He could ever depart. It was rooted in what God is, not in what man is.

Israel has a great future. Scripture promises a day when as a nation the Jewish people will look to Christ in repentance and faith, and so enter with the Gentiles into a New Covenant (Zech. 12:10; Rom. 11:26).

The promises by God to Israel were both spiritual and

physical. They included land. The repeated predictions concerning Israel's future cannot be other than literal. Jeremiah 29:11 says, " 'For I know the plans I have for you,' declares the Lord, 'plans to prosper you and not to harm you, plans to give you hope and a future.' " Hosea 3:5 promises, "Afterwards the Israelites will return and seek the Lord their God and David their king. They will come trembling to the Lord and to his blessings in the last days." Ezekiel 36:24 reinforces God's future purposes for Israel: " 'For I will take you out of the nations; I will gather you from all the countries and bring you back into your own land.' "

Is not this Israel's literal preservation and ultimate restoration? There is no other way to explain how these people have returned to their own land three times — from Egypt, from Babylon, and now from the ends of the world. Such a happening is unique in world history.

All Israel Will Be Saved

Paul asks the question in Romans 11:1, "Did God reject his people?" The Apostle answers his own question under divine inspiration in verse 2 of the same chapter: "God did not reject his people, whom he foreknew." His claim then is that Jews can believe and be saved. Paul is a living example of this fact. He says, "I am an Israelite myself" (Rom. 11:1). Furthermore, verse 5 of chapter 11 clearly tells us that there will always be Jews who believe: "At the present time there is a remnant chosen by grace." The sovereign God who has chosen the Church — His bride — has also chosen Jews in this Gentile age. But that is not all. There is something more exciting to follow. All Israel is to be saved. When? When "the full number of the Gentiles has come in. And so all Israel will be saved, as it is written. 'The deliverer will come from Zion; he will turn godlessness away from Jacob' " (Rom. 11:25-26).

When Paul says that all Israel will be saved, he means a remnant of the nation. "He who scattered Israel will gather them' " (Jer. 31:10); to dwell in Judah itself (Jer. 31:24); she is to be brought to the blessing of the New Covenant (Jer. 31:33); because then they will all know me from the least of them to the greatest (Jer. 31:34).

We know it will only be a remnant because the prophet Zechariah in states of that time in the Tribulation: " 'In the whole land,' declares the Lord, 'two-thirds will be struck down and perish; yet one-third will be left in it' " (Zech. 13:8).

Furthermore, we also highlight the consistent approach by God in His dealings with the Jew. Under the terrible reign of the Russian dictator Joseph Stalin, from 1929 to 1953, two-thirds of Russian Jewry perished. During the Holocaust, between 1933 and 1945, two-thirds of Jews perished under the German dictator Hitler.

So we have the promise of a revival in the Holy Land such as has never been seen before. That revival will be complete after the Great Tribulation, at the time when Christ comes to reign for 1,000 years upon this earth. But why that generation? Simply because the Lord is sovereign. Why has any generation seen revival? We are not privy to that information, but like the apostle Paul we can do no better than to acknowledge the greatness and glory of Almighty God (Rom. 11:33-36).

15. Question: Why doesn't Israel see itself in prophetic Scriptures?

Answer: In earlier days this question often puzzled me. After all, the Scriptures are very plain as to the role of Israel during the Tribulation. The clear purpose of the Tribulation is the out-pouring of God's wrath on a disbelieving and heart-hardened Israel. The answer to this question can be found in an amazing prophecy in the Book of Hosea.

In chapter 3:4-5, we have a prophecy which was written over 2,600 years ago, but it describes in exact detail the situation of the Jewish people and the nation of Israel today:

"For the Israelites will live for many days without king or prince, without sacrifice or sacred stones, without ephod or idol. Afterwards the Israelites will return and seek the Lord their God and David their king. They will come trembling to the Lord and to his blessings in the last days."

The interesting phrase in the passage is *"many days,"* and is translated in the Hebrew as *"yamim rabbim."* This is a Hebrew idiomatic expression denoting a long indefinite period of time. It specifically refers to the time of the Gentiles. Also inherent in this prophecy is the indestructibility of the Jew. The Jew will continue to exist. He cannot and will not be destroyed by satanic-inspired anti-Semitism or through social or religious assimilation.

What does the prophecy tell us about Israel?

It states in general that Israel will always exist, but specifically it tells how the Jewish people will live under the domination of the Gentile nations. The prophet declares that they will live for "many days" without: 1) king and prince, 2) sacrifice and sacred stones, 3) ephod or idol (teraphim).[4]

The king, sacrifice, and the ephod have all been given to Israel by God. They are God's choice for her. The prince, the sacred stones, and teraphims on the other hand were Israel's response to God's choice and are therefore the people's choice. Now the prophet says, in effect, that during the time of the Gentiles, Israel will exist without choice, either God's choice or their own choice. United Israel has not had an earthly king since the days of Solomon (931 B.C.). They also rejected God's choice for King — His Son Jesus, preferring Rome to rule over them. As a result they have been under the domination of the Gentile nations. They have been without sacrifice since the temple was destroyed by the Roman general Titus in A.D. 70. Thus, Israel lost its God-given way of salvation or approach to Him, which was by blood sacrifices, as laid down in the Book of Leviticus.

Hosea also says neither will there be an image. The Babylonian captivity cured Israel of her idolatry, but the Jewish people still continue to search for God through the rituals and traditions of Judaism to this day. Hosea also states that they would be without ephod and teraphim. The ephod is a reference to the Urim and Thummim, whereby the high priest could discern God's will while judging Israel (1 Sam. 23:9-12, 30:7-8).

In contrast to this were the teraphim, or the false gods, from which the people sought to divine God's will. This part of Hosea's amazing prophecy has been completely fulfilled, but the prophet does not conclude at this point. Verse 5 explains what will happen after the time of the Gentiles has been fulfilled. When the *many days* have been completed, the nation of Israel will return and seek the Lord their God and David their king. When they do, the king, the priest, and the prophet will be restored to them. Jesus will return and be Israel's king.

When might this happen?

Maybe Hosea 6:2 gives us a clue. The prophet says: "After two days he will revive us; on the third day he will restore us, that we may live in his presence."

Perhaps we may apply with extreme caution the application that one day is with the Lord as a thousand years, and a thousand years as one day (2 Pet. 3:8). If so, it could be that as almost 2,000 years of Jewish history have expired since the Messiah was rejected, on the "*third day*" He will raise up the nation of Israel, even as He was raised up from the grave.

Time is rapidly drawing to a close. Most of the Jews today are blind to the fact of their significance in prophetic history. Very soon, however, their eyes will be opened as they are projected into the spotlight of Christ's fore-ordained blessings during the Millennium.

16. Question: What is the origin of the Star of David?

Answer: History does not reveal exactly when and why this six-pointed geometrical figure, became Judaism's national and religious symbol. Some sources suggest its origin

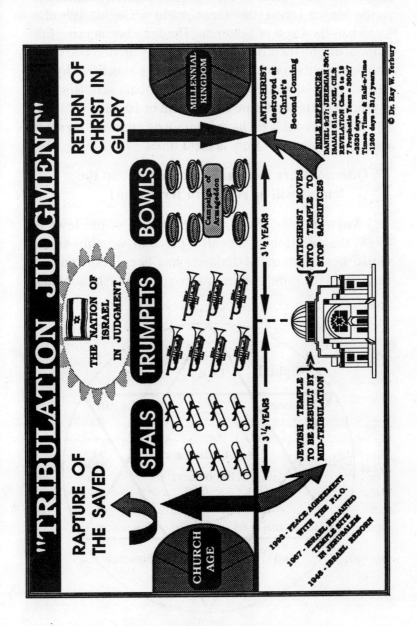

Chart 4: Tribulation Judgment

comes from Egyptian mythology. It is correctly referred to as the Magen David (the star or shield of David). It is also known as the Crest of Solomon. The Jews began using this symbol during their Babylonian captivity around 600 B.C., and has now become the Jewish symbol, sanctified by the Jewish people, and considered by Kabbala scholars as a mystic sign for the future redemption of Israel.

The stars of David have been found engraved on stone and other ornaments from ancient times.

17. Question: Are there any recent signs that the temple will be rebuilt in Jerusalem?

Answer: Yes! Ever since the return of the Jews in 1948, the question of a central place of worship as the world headquarters of Judaism has been very much a priority in the minds of the *yeshiva* (the Jewish rabbinate

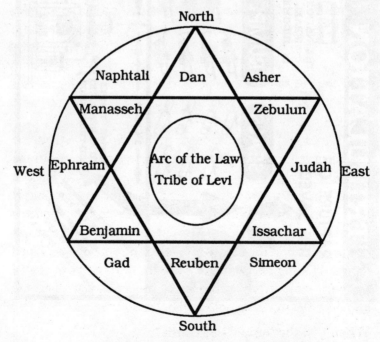

Diagram 2: The Star of David

training school), and the religious leaders.

More recently there has been a degree of urgency by the Ministry of Religion to gather information from Jews around the world regarding plans, availability of materials, and finances to pay for such a construction. The consensus of opinion is strongly in favor of building the third temple on the site of Solomon's Temple located on Mount Moriah.

What about the Moslem's "Dome of the Rock"?

On the surface, this structure would appear to be a huge stumbling block to any construction other than Arab buildings. I am told, however, that discussions have taken place among top Jewish and Arab authorities on this subject. After all, they say, we do worship the same God!

There is another school of thought that postulates Islam's holy place — the Dome of the Rock — is built outside and to the south of the temple site, and as such there is nothing hindering the future construction of the temple. That argument may satisfy the Jewish religious leaders, however, politically, such a scenario would present insurmountable problems, even in the present climate of "peace at any price." Quite apart from all the conjecture, the biblical fact is this: The temple will be rebuilt in spite of any obstacle on God's Holy Mountain.

We cannot guarantee peace in the Middle East, but we can be certain His temple will stand one day in place of the Moslem Dome of the Rock. The first temple was built in Jerusalem and was known as Solomon's Temple. Zerubbabel built an inferior temple on the mount after the Jews returned from captivity in Babylon. The Maccabees started restoration work on a badly deteriorated temple, but never finished the work. King Herod demolished the site and built one of the most magnificent buildings of the times. This became known as Herod's Temple or the Second Temple.

When will the temple be rebuilt?

The prophet Daniel reveals several facts about the third

temple to be built on Mount Moriah.

1. It must be in operation by no later than the middle of the Tribulation (Dan. 9:27).

2. It will be a physical structure.

3. The Antichrist will occupy the temple at the mid-point of the Tribulation. At such time he will: a) put an end to the Jewish sacrifice, b) all offerings (gifts) will cease, and c) he will cause an abomination. Could it not be the image that speaks will be set up in the temple, and demand that mankind worship the beast? (Rev. 13:14-18; 2 Thess. 2:4).

Today the Jewish religious authorities in Jerusalem are making every preparation to rebuild the Jewish temple on the same parcel of land the original temple was built on.

The completed plans are stored in a building in the Jewish quarter of the Old City. The model of the temple is housed at the Temple Institute in Jerusalem. The gold, silver, and copper vessels to be used in temple worship are fabricated and available for use. They are not museum pieces. The writer has had the rare privilege of handling and photographing the complete range of vessels.

There are numerous priestly schools called *"yeshivas"* where young Jewish men are being trained in all aspects of the laws of the priests as they pertained in ancient temple times. Many who attend these schools scattered throughout the old city of Jerusalem are *Cohanims* (priestly descendants).

The building materials will all be available from within Israel when required. After all, there is enough stone and rocks in the whole land to build many temples. The cornerstone for the temple today lies just outside the walls of the Old City. This huge piece of stone cut by hand from a quarry near the southern town of Beersheba, has been a source of trouble ever since Gershon Salomon, founder and director of the Temple Mount and Land of Israel Faithful, attempted to bring it through the Dung Gate and onto the Temple Mount in the late eighties. Perhaps one day this very stone will play a significant role in the final hours of world history.

There is also a big educational drive among school children throughout Israel, using models of the temple to explain the full meaning of temple worship. It is generally accepted that their motivation is educational and peaceful, and in no way political.[5]

The tragedy of the Jews' current philosophy is that they want *a* temple instead of *the* temple, so that *a* Christ (this will be the Antichrist) can seat himself in the Holy Place instead of *the* Christ.

Note: Refer to question 77, page 183, for an in-depth look at the importance of the Temple Mount in Bible prophecy and world history.

Table 1. Important Historical Dates

Note: Dates supplied as approximate guide only

2000 B.C. — Abraham leaves Ur
1450 (?) — Exodus of Hebrews from Egypt
1000 Reign of King David in Jerusalem
931 — The divided kingdom
722/21— The Assyrian captivity of Israel
612 — Fall of Nineveh
605 — The Battle of Carchemish
606/86 — The Babylonian captivity of Judah
539 — Fall of Babylon
539 — The Decree of Cyrus
538-444 — Return (three) of the exiles
440 (?) — The last word from the Old Testament.
470-300 — The rise of the Greek Philosophers
334 — Alexander invades Macedon
325 — The rise of the Ptolemaic Empire
320 (?) — The rise of the Seleucid Empire
200 (?) — The Septuagint translation begins
165 — Maccabean revolt
64 — Pompey conquers Jerusalem
31 — Reign of Augustus Caesar

6/5 — Birth of Jesus Christ
30/32 — Crucifixion
A.D. 70 — Jerusalem taken, temple destroyed
100 — Death of the last apostle — John
400 — The rise of the papacy
622 — The rise of Islam
1517 — Martin Luther and the Reformation
1620 — Pilgrims set sail for America
1730 — The Wesleyan Revival
1860 — Birth of Theodor Herzl
1917 — Balfour Declaration
1948 — Proclamation of Jewish State
1963 — Six Day War
1973 — Yom Kippur War
1993 — Peace Accord with Palestine (P.L.O.)
1994 — Israeli-Jordanian Peace Agreement

18. Question: Does Jerusalem belong to the Jewish people, or should it be an "international" city?

Answer: Since independence in 1948, Jerusalem first lived a divided existence for 19 years, but since the Six-Day War in 1967 the city has been reunited under Israeli administration. However, many people and governments, including the papacy, insist that solution to the "Middle East problem" will not be possible until Israeli Jews relinquish their "occupation" and restore the Holy City, or at least give back the eastern section to its rightful owners, the Moslem Arabs.

Are Moslems the rightful owners?

Prior to the 1967 Six-Day War, claims to Jerusalem being a Moslem holy city were rare. As a point of fact, Jerusalem has always been a city in which many religions and nationalities existed side by side with respect for each other's differing practices and beliefs.

The notion to call Jerusalem an Islamic holy city has

only come about in recent times, mainly since the defeat of the Jordanians who occupied Jerusalem prior to 1967. Furthermore, since the signing of the peace accord between Israel and the P.L.O. in September 1993, the idea has surfaced in the minds of many governments that making Jerusalem an international city would bring peace and stability to the region in general and Israel in particular.

Moslem Arabs, particularly from the more militant governments do not agree. They believe that a *"jihad"* or holy war should be declared to bring the city back into Arab possession.

What is the basis of their claim?

The only basis for such a claim is that Jerusalem contains an Islamic holy site, namely the Temple Mount (sacred to both Moslems and Jews) with its two mosques, El Aksa and the Dome of the Rock. This is the place from which Mohammed is believed to have ascended in a night journey to heaven.

Despite claims to the contrary their is *no evidence* that Mohammed ever set foot in Jerusalem. Aware that it was a holy city for both Christians and Jews, and wishing to convert them to his new religion, he commanded his followers to build a mosque in Jerusalem. The parameters for such a building was that it should be more glorious and a more splendid building than any of the churches and synagogues in the Holy City. Their claim is unfounded and tenuous.

Only on the basis of this religious tradition have the Moslems designated the entire Jewish Temple Mount to be their holy site, and the Israeli government has acceded to this tradition in a spirit of accommodation and good relations with the Moslem *Wakf* (the Supreme Moslem Council which maintains religious jurisdiction over Islamic holy places).

But Moslem Arab assertiveness doesn't end with the Temple Mount issue. On this tenuous claim, they have fabricated a claim to the entire city of Jerusalem. Although initially they would like the world to believe it's only the East Jerusalem sector they desire (which they have declared to be their "third holiest city") Mecca and Medina in Saudi Arabia, to which no "infidel" may visit, are the most sacred cities.

Jerusalem was never an Arab capital.

The city of Jerusalem — in contrast to Damascus, Cairo, or Baghdad — has never played any major role in the political and religious life of the Moslem Arab. It was never a political center, or a national or provincial capital. It was the site of one Moslem holy place, but otherwise a backwater to the Arabs. The passion for Jerusalem was not discovered by the Moslem Arab until most recent history.

As a point of fact, everything on the surface of the Temple Mount today is Moslem. Everything under the Temple Mount is Jewish.

Jerusalem is the city belonging to the Jews

Jerusalem has stood at the center of the Jewish people's national life and identity since King David made it the capital of his united kingdom around 1000 B.C. It remained that capital of a divided kingdom for a further 400 years until conquered by the Babylonians in 586 B.C.

After the return from Babylonian exile, Jerusalem again served as the capital of the Jewish people for the next 600 years, until its sacking in A.D. 70 by the Roman general Titus.

Jews are not squatters in a foreign land. They are not usurpers in the city of David — Jerusalem. They have been living there since the biblical era and have been the major population since the nineteenth century.

What is often overlooked is the biblical fact that Abraham paid for a parcel of land (Gen. 23:16-18) even though God gave him the land of Canaan under the covenant as outlined in Genesis 12-13,15,17,22,26. Furthermore, King David paid cash money for the Temple Mount when he bought the threshing-floor from Araunah the Jebusite as recorded in 2 Samuel 24:24.

Jews have property, synagogues, and other holy sites in most cities of the world. But do they claim sovereignty over those cities because of it? Of course not! It would be preposterous and people wouldn't accept such action. The Moslem Arab claim to Jerusalem, based on the mosques on the Temple Mount, is just as untenable.

Jerusalem has been the center of Jewish life, culture, religion, and education for over 3,000 years. That is the reason the state of Israel has recently rededicated the Jewish holy city to be its indivisible capital, the city of the Jews. It is also the city of the Great King, the Royal city, the city to which Jesus came and gave His life, the city to which He will one day return to firstly protect His chosen race the Jews from the Antichrist, and finally to reign as King of kings and Lord of lords.

Zechariah the prophet had this to say about Jerusalem:

"On that day, when all the nations of the earth are gathered against her, I will make Jerusalem an immovable rock for all the nations. All who try to move it will injure themselves" (Zech. 12:3).

"Then the leaders of Judah will say in their hearts, 'The people of Jerusalem are strong, because the Lord Almighty is their God' " (Zech. 12:5).

"On that day I will set out to destroy all the nations that attack Jerusalem" (Zech. 12:9).

19. Question: Should Israel exchange land for peace?

Answer: Never before in the history of the ancient and modern world have we had such an incessant call for peace by world leaders. Today many countries across the globe want peace, and Israel is no exception. It wants peace after 47 years of war and tension since nationhood in 1948. This is an understandable and responsible aim. However, in reality, is peace possible in a world which has clearly rejected the Prince of peace — the one who can and will bring everlasting peace, but only when He returns to planet Earth?

A former president of the Norwegian Academy of Science, assisted by historians from Britain, Egypt, Germany, and India, and with the aid of a powerful computer, has found that since 3600 B.C. the world has known only 292 years of peace. In this same period of more than 55 centuries, there have been 14,531 wars, both large and small, in which more than 3.6 billion people have been killed. Since 650 B.C. there have been 1,656 arms races of which only 16 have not ended in war. Nevertheless, those 16 particular countries did experience economic collapse.

Dividing Up the Land

Not only the Moslem countries, but in fact all the nations of the world are united in calling for the division of the land of promise. Every nation who is a signatory of the U.N. (excluding Israel and the USA who abstained) has endorsed U.N. Resolution 242, the basis for the current peace negotiations, which paraphrased says that: "Israel shall live in peace with her Arab neighbors when she returns to the pre-1967 borders."

This means dividing up the land once again and most importantly, dividing up the city of Jerusalem as it was from 1948 to 1967.

But the Bible indicates that such an action will result in judgment on those nations that call for such a division. Joel 3:2 says: " 'I will gather all nations and bring them down to the Valley of Jehoshaphat. There I will enter into judgment against them concerning my inheritance, my people Israel, for they scattered my people among the nations and divided up my land.' "

The PLO Charter Is to "Phase Out" Israel

Despite the fact that the nations of the world are united

on the issue of dividing up the land of Israel, such action is actually playing right into the hand of Yassir Arafat. He has stated through Adu Jihad, his deputy at the Algiers PLO summit in 1988, "What we are doing is carving out a two-phase strategy. First we get a Palestinian state next to Israel, then we use it as a base to destroy what remains of Israel."

Now you would be justified in saying that all this has changed since the Washington Summit in September 1993. After all, the whole world was witness to the famous handshake between Rabin and Arafat on the lawns of the White House! The PLO wants peace!! But do they?

After the signing ceremony one of the conditions placed on Arafat was that he would get the PLO Covenant changed to remove the words calling for the destruction of Israel. However, to date he has been unable to convince the PNC (Palestinian National Council) to do this. What causes the most worry is that Israel turns a blind eye to this major issue.

It seems the leaders of the Knesset (Israel's Parliament), or more particularly Prime Minister Rabin, are willing to ignore the plain fact that leopards never change their spots. We see, almost on a daily basis, dialogue and negotiations with an international terrorist organization — the PLO and its chairman Arafat — to exchange land for peace. But it won't succeed.

The Land of Israel Belongs to God, Not Man

When God took His people out of Egypt under Moses, He led them to Mount Sinai and there instructed them how to live as a community of chosen people. He gave them 613 rules and laws. God also instructed them how they should care for the land of Canaan. This is what the Bible says: "The land must not be sold permanently, because the land is mine and you are but aliens and my tenants" (Lev. 25:23).

God also said to Abraham: "All the land that you see I will give to you and your offspring for ever" (Gen. 13:15).

Israel is God's land to give and man's to receive.

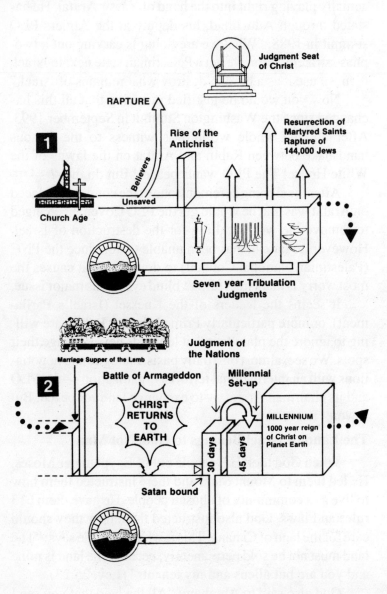

Chart 5: The End of this Age

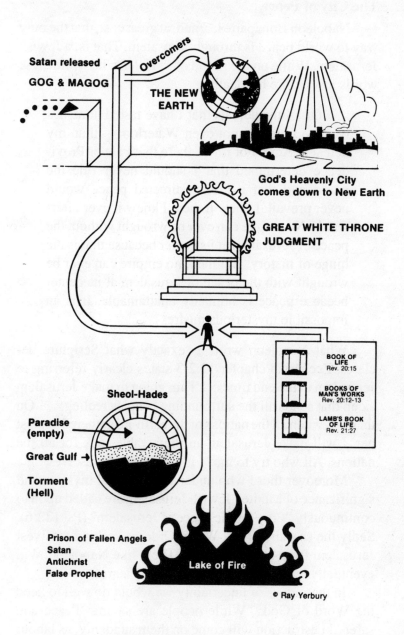

The Beginning of a New Era

The City of Peace

Napoleon Bonaparte learned, at great cost, that the only way to world peace is through Jerusalem. That is, a Jewish Jerusalem. While on the island of St Helena, he wrote these words just before his death:

> Of all the defeats that I have tasted none has been so bitter — not even Waterloo — than my defeat at Acre. For it was there that Fate or Providence determined that I should never rule the world and that a French-directed peace would never prevail. I knew it then. I knew it ever afterwards. No empire can ever be wrought without the peace of Jerusalem at its center because that is the hinge of history. But then, no empire can ever be wrought with the peace of Jerusalem at its center because peace is humanly unattainable. It is an impossible mysterious mistress.

What Napoleon wrote is exactly what Scripture declares. Zechariah chapter 12:2-3 states clearly referring to Jerusalem in the end times: " 'I am going to make Jerusalem a cup that sends all the surrounding peoples reeling. . . . On that day, when all the nations of the earth are gathered against her, I will make Jerusalem an immovable rock for all the nations. All who try to move it will injure themselves.' "

Moreover those who understand the real mystery and significance of a united Jewish Jerusalem are called upon to continuously "Pray for the peace of Jerusalem" (Ps. 122:6). Sadly the so-called New World Order is seeking to divest Jerusalem from Jewish control. They, like Napoleon, will eventually learn the hard lesson that he learnt.

In these days of uncertainty we would do well to heed the Word of God: "While people are saying 'Peace and safety,' destruction will come on them suddenly, as labour pains on a pregnant woman, and they will not escape" (1 Thess. 5:3). I believe we live in such a time.

4

The Church Age

20. Question: What is the divine purpose of the present Church Age?

Answer: Since Israel's rejection of the King, and hence the Kingdom, God has revealed a mystery which in the past was not made known (Eph. 3), and that is, namely, to take out from among the Gentiles, "a people for himself."

James says, " 'Brothers, listen to me. Simon has described to us how God at first showed his concern by taking from the Gentiles a people for himself' " (Acts 15:13-14).

This was in no way to replace God's kingdom program for Israel, but in view of their rejection, to suspend the fulfillment until the divine purpose for the present age has been consummated (1 Thess. 4:13-17).

After this the King declares: " 'I will return and rebuild David's fallen tent. Its ruins I will rebuild, and I will restore it, that the remnant of men may seek the Lord, and all the Gentiles who bear my name,' says the Lord, who does these things that have been known for ages" (Acts 15:16-18).

The Church was born in supernatural power in Jerusalem at Pentecost. It was built upon the rock of Matthew 16:18: " 'And I tell you that you are Peter, and on this rock I will build my church, and the gates of Hades will not overcome it.' "

What was Jesus saying? Not that the Church would be

built upon Peter, as our Roman Catholic friends believe. Rather, Jesus was saying, "You are Peter — 'the pebble,' and I will build my Church on the Rock — 'Jesus Christ,' and nothing will interfere with My plans."

So here was to be a unique Jewish/Gentile assembly, made one in Christ, on equal terms of unmerited favor during the present age of the Church (Col. 1:26-27; Eph. 2:11-18). The Church Age is the period of Christ's concealed glory. The Millennium will be the period of the manifestation of Christ's glory.

But — the Church will cease to exist after the Rapture, simply because the great Church victorious will be the Church at rest, in the presence of the glorified Son of God — for ever and ever.

21. Question: What does the expression "the time of the Gentiles" mean? What event concludes this period of history?

Answer: This phrase appears in the Gospel of Luke 21:24. The term "fullness of the Gentiles" appears in Romans 11:25. The former refers to the era of Gentile world domination, which commenced with the ascendancy of Nebuchadnezzar, and will terminate with the return of Jesus Christ to reign on this earth. The Scofield Reference Bible lucidly defines this time limit:

> The times of the Gentiles is that long period beginning with the Babylonian captivity of Judah under Nebuchadnezzar and will conclude with the destruction of the Gentile world-power by the "stone cut out without human hands" (Dan. 2:34,35,44). This refers to the coming of the Lord in power and great glory (Rev. 19:11). Until this time is decreed in the mind of our sovereign Lord, Jerusalem is politically subject to Gentile rule.[6]

As the time draws closer to the end, the Bible predicts

a world in chaos. We are certainly being conditioned today with ever increasing problems that man seems unable to solve. The Bible predicts a bleak future of disasters on a scale never before imagined, with men's hearts failing them from fear as they contemplate international confusion and economic crisis.

The Bible confirms that this "mystery of iniquity" is already at work (2 Thess. 2:7), but cannot reach its zenith until the Church is taken out of the world in what is generally referred to as the Rapture of the Saints. With the Church removed, Satan's superman will emerge — the Antichrist. He will be the head of a 10-nation confederacy, or the commander-in-chief of the European Empire.

When the fullness of the Gentiles is reached God's time clock will re-commence with the Rapture of the saints and the Tribulation.

22. Question: Are the Rapture and the Second Coming identical events?

Answer: I have found over the years that people become confused with the two stages of Christ's return. NO! They are not identical. They are two separate events, the former preceding the latter by a seven year period.

The word rapture means "in a state of being carried away with joy, love, and pleasure, resulting in ecstasy." Scripture certainly supports that this event will be a great joyous occasion when the Bride (Church) and Bridegroom (Christ) are united.

When Christ came the first time He did so as the suffering servant. He only comes a second time when He stands upon the Mount of Olives (Zech. 12:4). The Rapture takes place in the air (1 Thess. 4). The Second Coming happens on earth.

Comparison: Rapture and Second Coming

1. The Rapture is a meeting with the Lord. The Second

Coming is a mission of the Lord.

2. The Rapture takes place in the air. The Second Coming happens on this earth.

3. The Rapture will be noisy for the believer. The Second Coming will be silent for the unbeliever.

4. The Rapture will take the world by surprise. At the Second Coming the world will mourn.

5. At the Rapture believers will have a glorified body. At the Second Coming all unbelievers will perish.

23. Question: Will the Church be caught up before or after the Tribulation?

Answer: For those who believe in the Rapture, there are three major schools of thought:

(a) Pre-tribulationists.
(b) Mid-tribulationists.
(c) Post-tribulationists.

The Pre-tribulation View. This is the view held by a large number of Christians. The Rapture of the Church will not only be pre-millennial (before the millennial reign of Christ) but pre-tribulational — i.e., the Church will not experience the severe period of suffering during the Tribulation.

The Post-tribulational View. These people agree with the pre-tribulation view that the Rapture will be pre-millennial, but hold that it will occur after the Great Tribulation: i.e., the Church will be on earth during the seven-year period of God's judgments.

The Mid-tribulational View. People of this view also agree that the Rapture will be pre-millennial, but say that it will occur at the midpoint of the Great Tribulation: i.e., the Church will experience only the first three and one-half years of the Tribulation. They will escape the period of severe suffering under the bowl/vials judgment.

There is an abundance of biblical references that clearly

teach believers (or the true Church) that they will NOT go through the Tribulation judgment — that period of time when God will pour out His wrath on a degenerate and sinful world.

The following points explain why the Church will not go through the Tribulation

1. The promised exemption from trial — Scripture clearly teaches that believers will be kept from the "time of trial" (Rev. 3:10). This verse is consistent with the blessed hope of Titus 2:13-14: "While we wait for the blessed hope — the glorious appearing of our great God and Saviour, Jesus Christ, who gave himself for us to redeem us from all wickedness and to purify for himself a people that are his very own, eager to do what is good."

2. Safety from the wrath of God — Many verses point to the fact that His bride — the Church — will not suffer the Tribulation wrath.

> For God did not appoint us to suffer wrath but to receive salvation through our Lord Jesus Christ (1 Thess. 5:9).

> Since we have now been justified by his blood, how much more shall we be saved from God's wrath through him! (Rom. 5:9).

> If this is so, then the Lord knows how to rescue godly men from trials and to hold the unrighteous for the day of judgment (2 Pet. 2:9).

Other promises given to the Church that assure us safety from the wrath of God are found in 1 Thessalonians 1:10; Joel 2:28-31; Malachi 4:2; and Zephaniah 1:14-18.

3. The promise of an imminent hope — In all of Scripture the Lord has made it quite clear that His return could be at any time. His promise in John 14 implies an imminent possibility. The angel who spoke to the disciples after the Lord ascended to heaven also implied this imminent blessed hope (Acts. 1:11). The apostles Peter, James, John, and Paul all share the hope of the imminent return of the Lord.

> "Two men will be in the field; one will be taken and the other left. Two women will be grinding with a hand mill; one will be taken and the other left. Therefore keep watch, because you do not know on what day your Lord will come. But understand this: If the owner of the house had known at what time of night the thief was coming, he would have kept watch and would not have let his house be broken into. So you also must be ready, because the Son of Man will come at an hour when you do not expect him" (Matt. 24:40-44).

Other biblical references are John 14:3; James 5:8; Titus 2:12-13; and 1 John 2:28 and 3:2-3.

If the Rapture can only take place at the mid-point or the end of the Tribulation, then there is no basis for saying that Jesus can come at any time. We would therefore know when Christ is coming, and this is contrary to Scripture (Matt. 24:36). Importantly, if we can see Christ only after the Tribulation, it would be better to die before the Tribulation!

4. Revelation of the man of lawlessness — According to Daniel 9:27, the Antichrist will confirm a covenant (peace treaty) with the nation of Israel for seven years. It should be noted that it is the signing of this so called "peace pact" that will commence the seven-year Tribulation period, not the Rapture.

Now in the middle of the Tribulation — i.e., after three and one-half years — the Antichrist will stop or put an end to Jewish sacrifices in the rebuilt temple located on Mount Moriah.

The Antichrist is the principal actor on earth during the seven-year Tribulation period. Now the apostle Paul says in 2 Thessalonians 2:1-10 that the Antichrist (or the lawless one) *cannot be revealed* until **he** has been removed from the world. Verses 7 and 8 says: "For the secret power of lawlessness is already at work, but the one who now holds it back will continue to do so till he is taken out of the way. And then the lawless one will be revealed, whom the Lord Jesus will overthrow with the breath of his mouth and destroy by the splendour of his coming."

Who Is "He?

Considerable confusion exists among many well-respected Christian teachers and leaders relative to the ministry of the Holy Spirit during the Tribulation period. Unfortunately, much of this confusion has originated from the footnote in the Scofield Reference Bible on 2 Thessalonians 2:1-12. This footnote indicates that the Holy Spirit, the restraining influence on Satan the devil, will be removed when the Church is raptured just before the Tribulation begins.

In verse 7, the restrainer, or "he is taken out of the way," is masculine, and thus would refer to a person or individual who presently withholds or hinders the revelation of Antichrist.

The Most Likely Interpretation

The Church is the temple of the Holy Spirit (1 Cor. 3:16; Eph. 2:21-22). When she is "caught up" or "raptured," the Holy Spirit, "He," will have lost His dwelling place here on this earth, and therefore will no longer have the vehicle (men and women) to oppose the forces of evil.

In Genesis 6:3 God declared, "My spirit will not always contend with man." At that time the Holy Spirit abandoned a perverted society who was then swiftly judged by the Flood. But the Holy Spirit did not disappear. He was still present then and He will be forever. He is eternal (Heb. 9:14).

We must also remember that the Holy Spirit is omnipresent (Ps. 139:7). Even after the departure of the Church, which is His temple, the Holy Spirit will still be working among mankind of good will. Scripture reveals that during the Tribulation period "He" — the Holy Spirit — will be poured out on Israel, resulting in her conversion to their Messiah (Isa. 59: 20-21; Ezek. 39: 29; Zech. 12:10). Now we know that during the same period, that is the period of the Great Tribulation, a large number that no one could count, from every nation, tribe, people, and language, will be redeemed from the earth. These people must be the Gentiles (Rev. 7:9,14).

Now it is impossible to believe in Christ without the aid of the Holy Spirit (1 Cor. 12:3). It will, therefore, be necessary for Him to continue at least a part of His ministry on earth during this time of judgment.

The Redeemed Multitude

Verse 9 of Revelation 7 then paints a small picture of a vast crowd of people who will be saved during the Tribulation period. If they are not redeemed from earth during this period, then where do they come from? If, on the other hand, they are redeemed from earth, but the Holy Spirit was absent, how then was it possible to obtain salvation?

The answer is quite simple. This mighty revival is a result of the power of God's Holy Spirit working through dedicated vessels — the 144,000 sealed Israelites already scattered around the world. The people from "all nations, tribes, and languages" indicate the extent and magnitude of this revival, and is rivaled only by the first-century moving of the Spirit of God, when "the gospel has been proclaimed to every creature under heaven" (Col. 1:23). However, there is one vital difference in this revival from that of the first century. During this Tribulation period every tribe will not only hear the gospel but will also have many of its members respond to salvation just prior to the return to this earth of Jesus Christ

We indeed should continually praise God for His unfailing love and mercy!

24. Question: What group of people will take part in the Rapture?

Answer: This question has been the subject of much debate and argument down through the ages. There are some "religious groups" who claim exclusive right to that event. To answer the question, we must define three terms often used incorrectly:

1. Religion: It is nothing more than a man-centered organization, manipulated by worldly leaders for their own self-centered, egotistical gain. The leaders of religion, both men and women, are power-hungry, money-grabbing, self-sanctimonious, and more than often evil. The Lord called them, "blind leaders of the blind" (Matt. 15:14; Isa. 2:22).

2. Denominations: These are part of the total religious scene. Once again, they are man-made structures. Quite often the expression is heard, "The Church is wrong on this or that issue." But, according to Scripture, the true Church cannot go wrong. It is the denominations — i.e., Baptist, Presbyterian, Episcopalian, just to name a few, that are often wrong at various points.

3. The Church: Once again we must distinguish between the true Church and the false church. The false church is a self-appointed ministry. For example, it preaches the message of peace without regard to the moral and spiritual conditions which are basic to peace.

The true Church is not an organization. It is an organism, because it grows from strength to strength. It is composed of people. The building is nothing more than a rain shelter, although many would find this concept difficult to grasp, particularly in light of the huge amounts of money

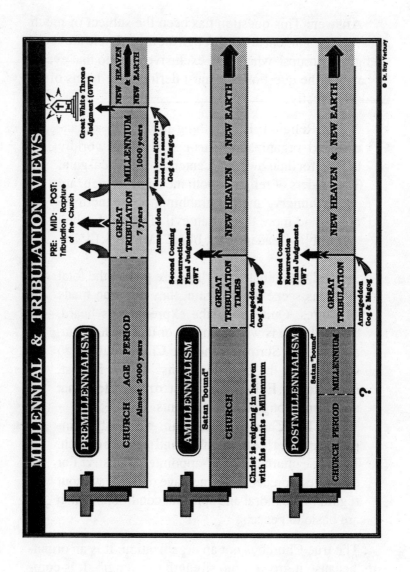

Chart 6. Millennial & Tribulation Views

some denominations spend to build man-made edifices.

The True Church

The Lord said, "I will build my Church." Therefore, to criticize the Church is to speak against the Builder. The Church that Christ was referring to was His elect, believers who are part of the body of Christ.

Ephesians 5:25-27 states: "Christ loved the church and gave himself up for her to make her holy, cleansing her by the washing with water through the word, and to present her to himself as a radiant church, without stain or wrinkle or any other blemish, but holy and blameless."

Who then will be Raptured?

1. Those who Belong to Christ. " 'I am the good shepherd; I know my sheep and my sheep know me' " (John 10:14).

The whole of the true Church will be raptured, because the Church is God's elect. Unfortunately, not all who claim to be Christians belong to the church of Jesus Christ. There are many religious people in church congregations who have never experienced the new birth. Our blessed Master once said, " 'Not everyone who says to me "Lord, Lord," will enter the kingdom of heaven' " (Matt. 7:21).

2. Those whose citizenship is in heaven. "But our citizenship is in heaven. And we eagerly await a Saviour from there, the Lord Jesus Christ, who, by the power that enables him to bring everything under his control, will transform our lowly bodies so that they will be like his glorious body" (Phil. 3:20-21).

This earth is only a stopping point for the believer. Here he is serving an apprenticeship to heaven — a sojourner in a foreign land. With this attitude, he should view everyday life from a heavenly point of view.

Our citizenship is in heaven, because, "God has raised us up with Christ and seated us with him in the heavenly realms in Christ Jesus" (Eph. 2:6).

3. Those who long for His return. "While we wait for

the blessed hope and the glorious appearing of our great God and Saviour, Jesus Christ" (Titus 2:13).

"So Christ was sacrificed once to take away the sins of many people; and he will appear a second time, not to bear sin, but to bring salvation to those who are waiting for him" (Heb. 9:28).

Our witness and discipleship for Christ should be a careful balance between working, watching and waiting. A waiting person is one who holds him or herself in readiness for the one for whom they are waiting.

4. Those who are purified. "Dear friends, now we are children of God, and what we will be has not yet been made known. But we know that when he appears, we shall be like him, for we shall see him as he is. Everyone who has this hope in him purifies himself, just as he is pure" (1 John 3:2-3).

Living a life of expectancy of Christ's imminent return demands a continual and ever-deepening purification on a daily basis.

5. Those who live a sanctified life. "It is God's will that you should be sanctified" (1 Thess. 4:3).

"Make every effort to live in peace with all men and to be holy; without holiness no-one will see the Lord" (Heb. 12:14).

The indispensable prerequisite for the child of God who wants to see the Lord is to live a life of holiness. Many people are satisfied to live a life of happiness. But holiness is the aim, happiness is the by-product.

At the Rapture there will be a great revelation. We will then know who belongs to the true church of Jesus Christ. Gone will be the denominations, for we will all be one in Christ. Today we see the foolishness of men wanting to make the church of Jesus Christ a united church through the Ecumenical movement. The true Church cannot be united by man. It is already a unity and complete. Only the walls of organizations divide it now. The revelation of the true church of Jesus Christ in all its splendor and glorified state will be breath-taking beyond description.

25. Question: What will the devil do when the Christians are taken to heaven?

Answer: While the Church is feasting with the Lord, the devil will be having a rare time on earth during the fulfillment of Daniel's seventieth week. That is the period of seven years when the Antichrist, energized by Satan, will make or confirm a covenant with the Jewish nation for that period. In the middle of the week of prophetic years, he will violate his pledge and then will commence the time of the greatest judgments this world has ever known.

At the mid-way point of the seven years of Tribulation, the whole of the evil trinity — Satan, the father; Antichrist, the son; and the false prophet, the mimic, who will copy the work of the Holy Spirit (Rev. 16:13) — will be consummated. The third person of this evil union — the false prophet — will cause the world to worship the Antichrist (Rev 13:4), and will have a mark prepared known as 666, and will require that people wear this identifying mark if they want to buy or sell during his reign.

The Scriptures show that this unprecedented period of world tribulation will be terminated by the arrival of Christ on earth. The Antichrist and the false prophet will be thrown into the lake of fire. Satan will be bound for 1,000 years (Rev. 20:1-6).

26. Question: What will happen to people left behind after the Rapture?

Answer: One of the big questions in people's minds is: "Will it be possible to be saved during the Tribulation period?" The removal of the Christians from planet Earth will precipitate the revealing of the Antichrist whose activities are confined to this seven-year Tribulation period.

The simple answer to this question is — **YES!**

Now, the people who are left behind at the Rapture are all non-believers. Many will be people who have attended church all of their lives. Unfortunately, attending church does not grant a passport into heaven.

Salvation to glory is obtainable after the Rapture, but must (will) be accomplished by persecution and martyrdom. This will occur during the first half of the seven-year Tribulation. Revelation 7:13-14 clarifies this point:

> Then one of the elders asked me, "These in white robes — who are they, and where did they come from?" I answered, "Sir, you know." And he said, "These are they who have come out of the great tribulation; they have washed their robes and made them white in the blood of the Lamb."

Due to the catastrophic events that will take place during this period, unbelievers who are killed will go to hades (hell). They will be held with all who have died as unbelievers since the world was created, waiting for the final Great White Throne judgment after the Millennium.

Now, at the mid-point of the Tribulation — after three and one-half years — Satan is thrown out of the heavenly realm (Rev. 12:7-12). This will cause him to vent his full fury on planet Earth. *The false prophet will emerge* and control the financial and commercial markets of the world. Anyone wishing to buy and sell during this period must receive the **mark of the beast — 666**.

At this point three things happen which will determine the people's destiny:

1. Anyone who receives the mark of the beast will immediately declare his allegiance to Satan by that action and will be put to death by Christ at His coming (Rev. 19:21).

2. Those who refuse the mark of the beast and are killed for their stand and witness for Christ will be raised at the "first resurrection" — at Christ's second coming (Rev. 20:4).

3. There will be many people located throughout the world, some in isolated places, who will not be directly involved or affected to a large degree by the wars surrounding the nation of Israel. These people will be judged when Christ returns at the judgment of the nations, also called the sheep and goat judgment (Matt. 25:31-46).

After all the frantic activity of the past seven years, finally a state of peace and calm will return to a somewhat altered planet (Zech. 14:3-5). On earth there will be no influence of the devil. Jesus Christ will reign with people in their fleshly human bodies together with the saints in their glorified bodies.

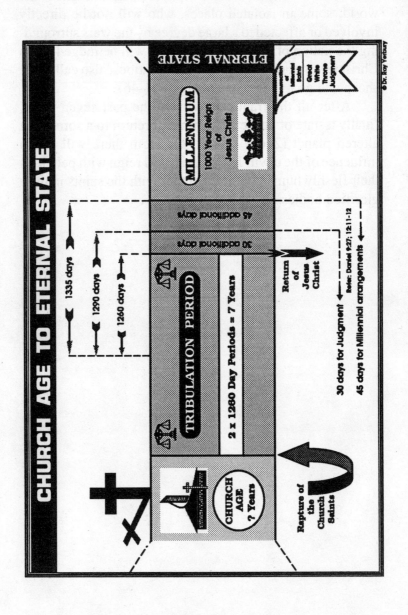

Chart 7. Church Age to Eternal State

5

Satan, the Antichrist, the False Prophet

27. Question: Satan is often dismissed as a figment of man's imagination. Is he real? Who are the demons we read about in the Bible?

Answer: Yes! Satan is very real.

The Bible is full of references to the *fact* of Satan. In Genesis 3:15 God declared war on Satan, and although Satan is claiming great victories in the lives of men and women today, Christ became the victor over Satan at the Cross. Eventually, he will be crushed and thrown into the lake of burning sulphur for all eternity.

We must be careful not to magnify Satan in our thinking and our theology. But at the same time it is dangerous to minimize him, because he is very real and very subtle. He is also powerful and probably more active today than at any other time in human history.

How do we know Satan is active?

1. The rapid growth in the occult.
2. The interest in spiritism.

3. The phenomenal birth-rate of new religions.

4. The spread of Islam.

5. Wide-spread apostasy within the professing Christian church.

Where did Satan come from?

In the Books of Ezekiel and Isaiah he is referred to as Lucifer — or the morning star (Ezek. 28; Isa. 14). He is a fallen angel — a super angel. Angels are created beings, created by God, and therefore totally subservient to Him. They are spiritual beings who minister on a spiritual plane. Fallen angels called demons can therefore be dealt with only on a spiritual plane with spiritual powers by spiritual people. These demons carry out Satan's evil instructions with plans to corrupt the world.

What are Satan's attributes?

1. He is a rational being — intelligent, subtle, wise.

2. He is not bound by space (Job 1:6).

3. He is immortal — not subject to death, but will be put to death in God's divine plan.

Satan is not:

1. Omnipresent. He cannot be in all places at the same time. Therefore he operates through legions of demonic forces — the fallen angels.

2. Omniscient. He does not know all things.

3. Omnipotent. He is not all powerful.

4. Satan does not possess the attributes of *Deity*. God created him and as such defines his boundaries, constraints, and power.

28. Question: Why is Satan so often depicted as an evil person in red clothes with horns sticking out of his head and a pitchfork in his hand?

Answer: This is exactly the image Satan would want people everywhere to have of him. Why? Because if people are looking for that image they will never find him, and thus he will be dismissed by the populace as a myth.

But Satan is not easily recognizable, and that is why so many people are deluded by him. We need to understand who he is and what he is doing. He hates Christians because of Christ, and uses every means possible to destroy them.

There are churches of Satan (satanism) in every major city of the world, meeting to pray and fast before the devil for the destruction of Christian families. He is our adversary, and as believers we are in the front line of a great spiritual battle from which there is no retreat.

The Devil is also known as:

1. The accuser. This is one of his major activities. He engages in false accusation and slander of God's people (Rev. 12:10).

2. The angel of light. Outwardly he appears very attractive and alluring, but inwardly he is diabolically destructive in every way.

3. The serpent. He is venomous, treacherous, and deadly. He moves silently, swiftly and subtly, watching and waiting for the moment to pounce and bite with deadly power. *Beware of him!*

29. Question: Will the Antichrist be an evil system or a real person? Is he alive in the world today?

Answer: There are a number of scholars who would say that Antichrist will only be a system, a pernicious system, an evil collective spirit which will be manifested at the end of time. However, these arguments are far from convincing as there are a large number of texts on the personality of the Antichrist.

No! He will be a real person, and I believe he is alive somewhere in the world today.

1. To the apostle John, he is very much a person (1 John 2:18,22; 2 John 7).

2. The apostle Paul is quite definite in his identification of the Antichrist as a person (2 Thess. 2:3-4).

3. Daniel is consistent in his reference to the same person as a king who shall pronounce words against the Most High, the one who shall oppress the saints and manipulate God's laws of nature (Dan. 7:24-26; 8:23-25; 9:27; 11:36-45).

Why I believe the Antichrist is alive today!

1. The rise and influence of false prophets and false doctrines.

Jesus warned His people that in the last days "false Christs and false prophets will appear and perform great signs and miracles to deceive even the elect — if that were possible" (Matt. 24:24). Not only are these false prophets more vocal today, but they seem to be gaining in religious power. This is one of the clear signs of the imminent return of Jesus Christ.

Many signs point to the fact that we are very close to the time of Christ's return. Considering the qualifications and maturity the Antichrist would need to possess in order to control a one-world government during the Tribulation, I believe he is already living among us, although unrevealed, just as the Lord Jesus was hidden for 30 years and then appeared publicly in the last three years of his life.

2. The incessant call for a world leader.

Many countries across the globe are in a hopeless economic, political, and religious mess. Increasingly the call goes out for a Messiah to come and solve their problems. Twelve European nations are working towards unity, and to some degree achieved that goal in the year 1992. The false priesthood represented in Catholicism is now losing its religious influence, but it is gaining more and more political power. Pope John Paul II is certainly a charismatic figure, a world traveler with worldwide political power. The Vatican is considered to be the richest government in the world.

3. Apostasy in the Christian church.

One of the clearest signs of Christ's imminent return is

the spirit of antichrist in the world. The apostle John prophetically described the situation as we have it today in 1 John 2:18-19. Ever-increasing numbers of *believers* are now becoming anti-Christian, even denying those fundamental truths of the Virgin Birth, the Resurrection, and the second coming of Christ.

Antichrist is alive in spirit and reality. Whom will you choose — Antichrist or Jesus Christ?

30. Question: When will this diabolical person called the Antichrist appear on planet Earth?

Answer: The simple answer is, after the Christians have been removed in the event called the Rapture (2 Thess. 2:7). But such a simple answer invokes another question: *Why* will the Antichrist appear after the Rapture?

It is a well-known fact that leaders of global significance have always appeared in the wake of international catastrophes. The sudden disappearance of say up to 5 percent of the current world population (approximately 300 million) will certainly head the list of all-time disasters.

History has shown that Napoleon would have gone down in the records as merely a great general but for the conditions of France after the French Revolution. Sir Winston Churchill became a great war leader. Why? Because of the crisis of the war in 1940. Most significant of all, Adolf Hitler would almost certainly have remained an obscure painter but for the state of Germany after the collapse of the Weimar Republic.

When we study in detail *"the man of sin"* or *"lawless one,"* as detailed in 2 Thessalonians 2 and Daniel 8, we note a striking similarity between the coming Antichrist and the infamous demagogue Hitler, except for one important difference. This man of sin will essentially be a man of peace (Dan. 8:25), who will rise to world prominence to restore law and order in the wake of the great disappearing millions from planet Earth.

So we see it will be in these circumstances that a genius of the caliber of the man of sin would gain immediate international status. He would rebuild from the ruins with dramatic effect. And like Hitler and Napoleon, he will be worshipped like a god, but to a far greater extent as the Bible indicates (2 Thess. 2:4)

31. Question: What is the mark of the beast — the mystical number 666?

Answer: The mark of the beast is discussed exclusively in Revelation 13:16-18. It has captured the imagination of mankind even to the extent that there are many people today who read a 666 on the Australian Bankcard, and because of this will not have anything to do with credit charging.

It is the mark of a system headed by the Antichrist, used to identify all people during the Tribulation period who worship and follow the beast.

Believers will not have to worry. Scripture is very clear about the mark. It is to be borne either on the forehead or in the palm of the right hand. It will be administered by the false prophet only from the halfway point during the Tribulation — i.e., after three and one-half years of the seven years of Tribulation.

People alive during the Tribulation will need to make a choice. The moment they take the mark, they seal their fate. There can be *no salvation* for those people who take the mark of the beast.

What does this number mean? The Bible says in Revelation 13:18, "If anyone has insight, let him calculate the number of the beast, for it is a man's number." In general, most scholars agree that the number **6** as applied to Scripture represents man. (Man was created on the sixth day, six days were allotted for man to work.)

Seven denotes completeness, but six implies incompleteness, always falling short. Now, as the Holy Trinity

(Father, Son, Holy Spirit) is the embodiment of godliness, so the embodiment of evil is manifested in a counterfeit trinity, *Satan, Antichrist, and false prophet.* It may also be that the beast will use the "6" three times to emulate God.

Who is this Antichrist? It is quite scriptural to apply wisdom to calculate the number of the beast (Rev. 13:18), but nowhere have we the authority to name him. We are not privy to his name. That will be revealed in God's timing. Unfortunately there are many people and groups who spend all their energies endeavoring to implicate different people. Hitler has been a candidate. The current pope, who is known as the "Vicar of Christ," is a popular target. Using letters from the Latin alphabet which have numerical values, his title *"Vicarius Filii Dei"* is made to add up to 666.

Surely we would do better to forget the fantasy and concentrate on the reality of God's Word.

32. Question: What is the difference between the two beasts of Revelation 13?

Answer: The first beast is referred to in Revelation 13:1-10. *He is the Antichrist.*

1. He arose out of the sea. The word "sea" is used in this context to mean that the Antichrist arises from among the people around the Mediterranean Sea.

2. He has 7 heads and 10 horns. The seven heads are seven mountains, which also symbolize seven kings dominated by the harlot Babylon (idolatry — Rev. 17:9). The 10 horns of Revelation 17:12 are the 10 kings which will make up the Antichrist's world confederacy of nations in the end times.

3. His head is adorned with names of blasphemy.

4. He will have a beast-like nature. This dictator's movement onto the world scene will be fast (leopard); he will be powerful (bear); he will be a distinguished person (lion).

5. He will be worshipped. This world leader will claim

to have been fatally wounded; will fake a resurrection; the world will be absolutely amazed; and this will cause people to worship him and Satan. Open satanic worship will characterize the "church" of the Tribulation.

6. He makes war with the saints and wins.

7. His activities are for 42 months.

8. He is finally destroyed by the Lamb. He goes into perdition, and is finally cast into the lake of fire (Rev. 19:20).

The second beast is referred to in Revelation 13:11-18 and is *the false prophet.*

1. He is the beast out of the earth. Alongside the first beast or the Antichrist, biblical prophecy places a person who will serve him as a sort of religious front man, a false prophet, a henchman to force the people into worshipping Antichrist.

2. He will have great influence. He will be the dictator's right-hand support. He will be the religious arm to the political leadership of the Antichrist — a real false prophet.

3. He will display awesome power. This pyrotechnic "cleric" will deceive millions into believing that he can save the world, which by now will be bursting at the seams if not a melt-down.

4. He will set up a "live" image of Antichrist. It is amazing how history tends to repeat itself. Nebuchadnezzar had an image set up in Babylon's main city square and demanded that it be worshipped. The false prophet will demand that people worship this image which has powers of speech. Could it not be computer-controlled?

5. He will control the economy of the day. The beast will have a mark prepared (666) that people will be required to wear if they want to buy or sell during his reign.

GREAT NEWS: This terrifying future is not for the child of God. While the beasts are on the rampage on earth, the believers or true Christians will be in heaven enjoying fellowship with the Bridegroom at the Marriage Supper of the Lamb.

Table 2
Contrast between Christ and Antichrist

Christ	Antichrist
1. Christ came from above (John 6:38).	**1.** Antichrist will ascend from the pit (Rev. 11:7).
2. Christ came in His Father's name (John 5:43).	**2.** He will come in his own name (John 5:43).
3. Christ humbled himself while on this earth (Phil. 2:8).	**3.** He will exalt himself when he comes to power (2 Thess. 2:4).
4. Christ was despised and rejected. (Isa. 53:3; Luke 23:18).	**4.** Antichrist will be admired (Rev. 13:3-4).
5. Christ will finally be exalted (Phil. 2:9).	**5.** He will be cast down to hell (Rev. 19:20).
6. Came to do His Father's will (John 6:38).	**6.** He will come to do his own will (Dan. 11:36).
7. Christ came to save the lost (Luke 19:10).	**7.** He will come to destroy the lost (Dan. 8:24).
8. Christ is the Good Shepherd (John 10:1-15).	**8.** He is the false (evil) shepherd (Zech. 11:16).
9. Christ is the "true vine" (John 15:1).	**9.** Antichrist is the "vine of the earth" (Rev. 14:18).
10. Christ is the "truth" (John 14:6).	**10.** He is the ultimate "liar" (2 Thess. 2:11).
11. Christ is the "holy one" (Mark 1:24).	**11.** He is the "lawless one" (2 Thess. 2:8).
12. Christ is the "man of sorrows" (Isa. 53:3).	**12.** He is the "man of sin" (2 Thess. 2:3).
13. Christ is the "Son of God" (Luke 1:35).	**13.** Antichrist is the "son of perdition" (2 Thess. 2:3).
14. He is the "mystery of godliness" (1 Tim. 3:16).	**14.** He will be the "mystery of iniquity" (2 Thess. 2:7).
15. He is the image of God (John 14:9).	**15.** He is the image of Satan (Rev. 12:3, 13:1, 17:3).

16. Christ is the second person of the Holy Trinity — Father, Son, Holy Spirit.

17. Christ has for His bride His church, holy and blameless, which He will raise with Him in glory (Eph. 5:25-27).

16. Antichrist is the second person of the evil trinity — Satan, Antichrist, false prophet.

17. The Antichrist has for a wife a prostitute, the apostate church, which he shall put to an end by burning (Rev. 17:1-16).

6
The Tribulation Judgments

33. Question: Why must there be a period of Tribulation on planet Earth? What purpose does it serve?

Answer: History demonstrates that the human race has been subjected to various judgments because of sin. There was the worldwide flood judgment. The cities of the plains — Sodom and Gomorrah were judged. But the most important past judgment to occur as far as mankind is concerned was the Calvary judgment. However, the Bible tells us that the most terrible epoch is still to come.

The seven-year "Tribulation judgments" will be horrible. Jesus himself warned that it would be greater than any past or future world judgment (Matt. 24:21).

Why must they take place? Simply because of **SIN**, and sin must be judged. There must be punishment for evil. The greatest sin is rejection of Christ. The Jews rejected the Messiah and had Him put to death. They even cried for His blood to be upon their children (Matt. 27:25), and that is why God will pour out His wrath upon the nation of Israel.

But God will not only judge Israel, He will also judge the sin of the Gentile nations. The might of the Russian forces will be destroyed on the northern hills of Israel (Ezek.

39:4). The forces of Antichrist, from the nations of the world, will be annihilated at the battle or campaign of Armageddon to take place on Israeli soil towards the end of this age (Rev. 16:12-16).

Finally, God's divine purpose will have been fulfilled. The judgments are complete. Now the earth can return to a state similar to that before sin entered the Garden of Eden. The first Adam departed from the Garden into the wilderness. The second Adam (Christ) came from the wilderness (Matt. 4) to go back to the Garden. At last, man will be able to enjoy intimate fellowship with his Creator, as was always originally intended.

34. Question: Who are the four horsemen of the Apocalypse? Are they men?

Answer: It is not God's intention to depict individual personalities through these horsemen, but rather "world conditions." The four horsemen present the picture of man's inhumanity to man. Each seal broken in heaven introduces a tragedy on earth.

1. The first seal (Rev. 6:1-2). We have the first of four horsemen, riding upon a **white horse.** You will observe that the horseman has a bow but no arrows, no fire power with which to inflict injury. Doubtless, this is a symbolic picture of the Antichrist as he initially, through diplomacy rather than weapons, subdues to himself the 10 nations of the revived Roman Empire. He will be successful as seen by the crown he wears on his head.

2. The second seal (Rev. 6:3-4). This is the rider on the **red horse** who has the sword of war. The uneasy peace which the rider on the white horse brings is only temporary. This rider now has the ability to "take peace from the earth and make men slay each other." Nations will revolt against the Antichrist's takeover of the world, but their attempts will be unsuccessful. The Antichrist, with his large sword (or arsenal of weapons), will at this time be triumphant.

3. The third seal (Rev. 6:5-6). Now we see the rider on a **black horse**. This third judgment brings famine to the world. Black is used to depict famine in other parts of Scripture (Jer. 4:28; Lam. 4:8-9). From past experience we know that famine often follows war, just as it did after World War I.

The balances in the hand of the rider on the black horse speak of inflation, a subject we have all been conditioned to this century. Food will indeed be scarce. The social security system, which acts as a buffer against starvation for the elderly and disadvantaged, will collapse. The rich, however, will not suffer to the same extent as the poor. The phrase "do not damage the oil and wine" would seem to indicate that the traditional luxury goods of the rich will somehow escape the rations, at least for part of the judgments. Once again the common people will bear the brunt of man's inhumanity to man.

4. The fourth seal (Rev. 6:7-8). The **pale horse** signifies death. It is the final link in the self-destructive chain for mankind. Literally one-quarter of the world's population, estimated in 1995 to be nearly six billion people, will die by the sword, famine, and the plague. Note that the wild beasts of the earth will not starve during this Tribulation period.

35. Question: Will the entire world be affected by the Tribulation judgments? Is it true that these judgments will be more severe on those nations who oppose Israel?

Answer: A study of the prophetic word, and in particular the Book of Revelation, reveals that even though the judgments of the Tribulation will be awesome, they will not be worldwide.

History has demonstrated quite conclusively that God has used evil nations who openly oppose Israel to judge His disobedient people. A typical example was the great Babylonian Empire under the reign of King Nebuchadnezzar.

Ultimately they were defeated and destroyed because of their pagan beliefs and practices. Egypt and its Arab allies is a recent example of God's protection of His people Israel, even though at present they choose not to recognize God's Son — Jesus Christ.

The nations that have supported and assisted Israel will be less affected than others, because they will come under the divine blessing of Genesis 12:3:

> I will bless those who bless you, and whoever curses you I will curse; and all the people on earth will be blessed through you.

On the basis of this same passage of Scripture, the nations that oppose Israel will come under God's curse, as indeed happened in the days of King Ahasuerus and Esther; that period of time just after the Babylonian captivity (Esther 9).

The Tribulation judgments will be confined to that area of our world around the European-Mediterranean nations where the main forces of the Antichrist will have assembled to attack Israel. The land of Israel will become a battlefield.

36. Question: There are a number of judgments in God's Word in addition to those of the Tribulation. What are they and when do they occur?

Answer: Jesus Christ is the judge of all people and nations. God the Father could quite easily have handled that task, but He has chosen to delegate that authority to His Son (John 5:19-29).

Of the 10 major judgments recorded in Scripture, three have already transpired, three are currently in progress, and four are future:

Past and present judgments:

1. The worldwide Flood judgment (Gen. 6).

2. The destruction of Sodom and Gomorrah (Gen. 19).

3. The judgment of the Cross — Satan defeated (John 16).

4. The self-judgment of believers (1 Cor. 11:31).

5. The judgment of carnal believers (1 Cor. 11:28-31).

6. The judgment of fallen angels (2 Pet. 2:4; Jude 6).

There are four future judgments:

1. The Judgment Seat of Christ (Bema). At the Rapture, all believers of the Church Age will receive their glorified bodies. This event takes place in the heavens — in outer space sometime around the mid-point of the Tribulation. Revelation 11:18 says: "The nations were angry; and your wrath has come. The time has come for judging the dead, and for rewarding your servants the prophets and your saints and those who reverence your name, both small and great — and for destroying those who destroy the earth." This passage of Scripture is talking about the judgment of believers, not unbelievers. Note the words used in chapter 11: "rewarding your servants." Some time after this event, but before the Marriage Supper of the Lamb, every believer must keep that appointment before the Judgment Seat, also known as the "Bema Judgment" (2 Cor. 5:10).

We should understand that the believers escape eternal perdition (eternity in the "Lake of Fire"), but their works as a disciple for Christ must be examined in order for rewards to be fixed. These rewards determine our responsibilities during the Millennium. For the undisciplined disciple or the worldly believer, it could mean the " loss of rewards" (2 John 8). Refer also to question 48.

2. The judgment of living Jews. The judgment of Israel will take place during the Tribulation and the nation will repent. There will also be a future judgment upon Israel when she is gathered from all nations to determine who will in that day, enter the kingdom blessing (Ezek. 20:34-38; Ps. 50:1-7; Mal. 3:2-5, 4:1-2).

3. The judgment of the nations. This is also known as the *sheep and goat judgment*. It is the judgment of all the individual Gentiles alive at the end of the Tribulation, and takes place on earth. It is probably that 30-day interval of time as outlined in Daniel 12:11. (Refer to chart 7, page 72.) The unsaved will be sent to eternal judgment; the saved (those without the mark of the beast) will enter the millennial kingdom which they now inherit in the fullest sense for 1,000 years (Matt. 25:31-46).

4. The Great White Throne Judgment. This is the judgment of the wicked dead. After the 1,000 years, a resurrection of all unbelievers will take place, somewhere in space. They will face the last great accounting, at which before the throne they will confess, whether they want to or not, Jesus Christ as Lord (Phil. 2:11). Their future is bleak, involving eternal separation from God (known as the second death) (Rev. 20:11-15).

37. Question: Who are the 144,000 people of Revelation 7? What is their purpose in Bible prophecy?

Answer: There has always been widespread confusion regarding the identity of these 144,000. Some church groups have made claims to their membership. The Jehovah's Witnesses have always maintained they are the ones, but as their numbers have increased so too has competition among their membership to ensure entry to this exclusive club.

However, the Scriptures could not be clearer. They are, as John states — **JEWS** — 12,000 from each of the 12 tribes. They will be sealed by God (Rev. 7:3) at the beginning of the Tribulation, and will go forth throughout the world to evangelize during the first half of the Tribulation. This will not happen until the true Church has been removed from the earth. As a result, a great soul harvest will be won to the Kingdom as detailed in Revelation 7:14.

It should be noted that the 144,000 of Revelation 14 are the same group as in Revelation 7. A number of this kind would not be used for two different groups in the same book.

Where are they as detailed in chapter 14?

They are now seen on heavenly Mt. Zion with the Lamb. Mt. Zion, as recorded in Joel 2:32, is the place of victory. The 144,000 have been redeemed from the earth, and have the "Father's name written on their foreheads" (Rev. 14:1).

38. Question: How will people be saved during the Tribulation if the Holy Spirit is removed with the Church at the Rapture?

Answer: This question has essentially been answered under question 23 on page 60. However, it is one that tends to both concern and confuse many people. They are concerned because their unsaved friends and relatives will be left behind at the Rapture of the true Church. They are confused because if the Holy Spirit is removed from the world, how can it be possible for salvation without the influence and activity of the third person of the Trinity? (1 Cor. 12:3).

The key passage of Scripture central to the removal of the Holy Spirit at the Rapture is found in 2 Thessalonians 2:7-8:

> For the secret power of lawlessness is already at work; but the one who now holds it back will continue to do so till he is taken out of the way. And then the lawless one will be revealed, whom the Lord Jesus will overthrow with the breath of his mouth and destroy by the splendour of his coming.

Now in verse 7 the restrainer, or "he is taken out of the way," is masculine and thus would refer to a person or individual who presently withholds or hinders the revelation of the person called the Antichrist.

A number of possible interpretations

1. The Holy Spirit. Since the work of the Holy Spirit is to convince (John 8:46) and to convict (John 8:9) men of sin, iniquity cannot reach its zenith until His removal. The restraining thing would then be the work of the Holy Spirit, which now acts as a divine dam holding back the flood of iniquity such as the world has never seen before.

2. The Church. As the Holy Spirit abides and dwells within the believer, and the believer constitutes the Church, therefore this body of believers in a sense exercises a restraining influence on the activities of Satan.

3. World governments or civil powers. There are some scholars who believe that this restraining influence refers to three of the kings of the European Empire who will restrain the Antichrist during the first three and one-half years of the Tribulation (Dan. 11).

Quite apart from this school of thought, a number of today's governments do strive to maintain some measure of law, order, and righteousness. Some governments have considerable Christian influence within their administration, and while this exists it is difficult to envisage the rise of the Antichrist.

4. The determinate counsel of Almighty God. Those who hold to this view say that the Antichrist will not be revealed on this earth until a time predetermined in the mind and will of God

The most logical and plausible interpretation as to the identity of the restrainer is as follows:

In summary: the Holy Spirit being omnipresent, but no longer indwelling the believer at this time will come upon a person during the Tribulation just as He did in Old Testament times, but then only in response to that person's acknowledgment of their need of a Saviour.

39. Question: Who are the two witnesses of Revelation 11?

Answer: Between Revelation 10:1 and 11:14 we have an interlude, a time-out period between the sixth and sev-

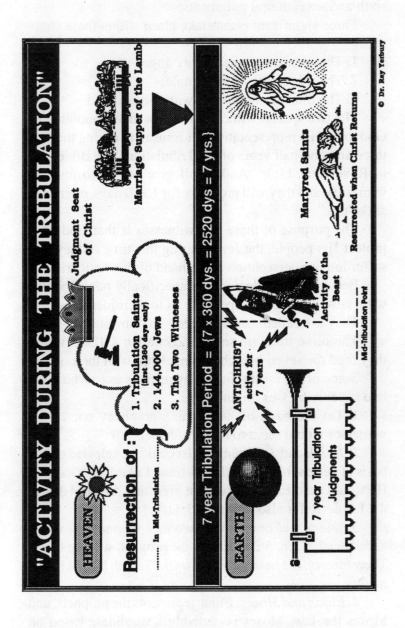

Chart 8. Activity during the Tribulation

enth trumpet judgment and similar to the one between the sixth and seventh seal judgments.

Three significant events take place within these chapters:

1. The message of the mighty angel;

2. The measuring of the temple;

3. The ministry of the two witnesses of God.

The two special witnesses are chosen and anointed by God to be His representatives in Jerusalem during the first three and one-half years of the Tribulation. The Bible says in Revelation 11:3: "And I will give power to my two witnesses, and they will prophesy for 1,260 days, clothed in sackcloth."

The purpose of these two witnesses is that God must protect His people, the Jews, during this time or they will suffer intense persecution at the hand of the Antichrist.

Because the Bible does not specifically name the two witnesses, we can only speculate as to their identities.

They are called: (a) olive trees; (b) lampstands.

The olive trees are seen in Zechariah 4:12-13 where they feed the seven-branched candelabra with their oil.

Some of the most reliable suggestions as to who these two super witnesses might be are:

1. On the basis of Zechariah's prophecy one of the witnesses would seem to be *Zerubbabel.*

2. *Elijah* and *John the Baptist* could be selected on the basis of verses from Malachi 4:5-6 and Luke 1:17. God said He would send Elijah before that great and dreadful day of the Lord. (Refer also to Matt. 17:11.)

3. *Enoch* was one of only two men who never experienced death (Gen. 5:24). Elijah, the prophet, was the other. Therefore, on the basis of Hebrews 9:27, both he and Elijah qualify.

4. *Elijah and Moses:* Elijah represents the prophets, and Moses the law. Moses is certainly a candidate based on Malachi 4:4-5. Elijah is again mentioned. Both Elijah and

Moses had powerful ministries. Both men appeared with Christ on the Mount of Transfiguration. and would be well-qualified to witness to the Jews in Jerusalem.

Now in Revelation 11 we note that the two witnesses die and are resurrected (Rev. 7:11-12). This would eliminate Moses, Zerubbabel, and John, because they have all died previously, and Scripture says that man can die only once (Heb. 9:27).

I believe the most likely answer is Elijah as the number one certainty, with Enoch the number two candidate. Many prophecy students believe that the great man Moses, who appeared with Elijah and the glorified Christ on the Mount of Transfiguration, is still a possibility.

We will just have to wait and see.

40. Question: What do the prophecies against Gog and Magog represent?

Answer: The prophecies against Gog and Magog have always presented problems as to their exact timing and meaning.

The Gog and Magog of Ezekiel 38 and 39 basically describe World War III; while on the other hand, Revelation 14, 16, and 19 describe the battle or campaign of Armageddon. Furthermore, the Gog and Magog referred to in Revelation 20 is that final revolt by the forces of Satan who has been released by God after the millennial reign of Jesus Christ. (Refer to chart 10, page 137.)

Now, most commentators agree that the description of Gog and Magog as recorded in Ezekiel 38 and 39 refers to the Russian world empire with its satellites in military attack mode. The Bible also indicated in Ezekiel 38:6,15; 39:2 that this great army will come from the far north. Moscow and the land of Russia is immediately north of Israel. In Ezekiel 38:3, the Bible says: " 'This is what the sovereign Lord says: I am against you, O Gog, chief prince of Meshech and Tubal.' "

Gog is the symbolic expression for "head" or "emperor" of all the Russians. *Magog* is also a symbolic expression for that country.

The Siberian or Asiatic capital of Russia was Tubal or Tobolsk, while the European capital was called Meshech. From the days of Napoleon it has been called Moscow.

Thus we see that Russia is clearly described in the Word of God and has been subsequently judged by God, because of its treatment of the Jews particularly under the military dictator Stalin, centuries before it was known by name.

41. Question: How do you relate the military hardware listed in Ezekiel 39:9 to modern day weaponry?

Answer: To adequately explain this question, it is necessary to consider other verses within both chapters 38 and 39 of Ezekiel.

In a most remarkable way, God was revealing through the prophet Ezekiel the future attempt by Russia — the country to the far north (Ezek. 38:6) to take over the new nation of Israel.

For this to happen, the prophecy is totally dependent upon there being a nation of Israel. At the time Ezekiel was given this word (580 B.C.), all Israel was in captivity. There was no established nation of Israel, and furthermore, as history has demonstrated, there was none for the next 2,500 years. Today's generation, however, has seen the birth of a new nation, and is quietly preparing itself for the onslaught from the military might surrounding its borders.

The recent political turmoil in Russia (1995), particularly regarding the way Boris Yeltsin and his gang of war psychotics have handled the Chechnya invasion is causing considerable concern and alarm in Israel.

In verse 4 of chapter 38 we read, " 'I will turn you around, put hooks in your jaws and bring you out with your whole army — your horses, your horsemen fully armed, and a great horde with large and small shields, all of them brandishing their swords.' "

The question that immediately arises from this reading is: "Will Russia attack Israel on horseback?" The answer is probably NO. If it were in Ezekiel's day the answer would be yes. Today we employ fast moving, powerful mechanized equipment such as tanks and armored personal carriers. This has taken the place of horses.

If God had told Ezekiel to write words like tanks, guns, rockets, and lasers, no one would have understood a word that was written until just 100 years ago.

Although Russia has many fine horses in their military establishment, her activities during the eighties in Afghanistan give clear evidence that the prophecy in Ezekiel is referring to modern day weaponry.

Verse 9 of chapter 38 is another example indicating that Russia will attack from the air: " You and all your troops and the many nations with you will go up, advancing like a storm; you will be like a cloud covering the land."

From this verse we see that Russia will strike by using a rapid deployment force, a tactic involving transport planes which can move complete armies very quickly.

However, for the student of Bible prophecy one continues to wonder with intriguing interest how this prophecy will all be fulfilled as today we watch on the sideline the self-destruction of the once mighty nation of Russia.

Now let us go back to our original question.

In Ezekiel 39:9 it says, " 'Then those who live in the towns of Israel will go out and use the weapons for fuel and burn them up — the small and large shields, the bows and arrows, the war clubs and spears. For seven years they will use them for fuel.' "

When we read this prophecy it is hard to imagine the Russian defense force using bows and arrows. That would be absurd. Well! What interpretation can be placed on this prophecy?

There is one school of thought suggesting that the

Russian military hardware is currently being manufactured out of a material called Lignastone, which is similar to laminated wood and burns slowly like coal. It has a greater tensile strength than steel, and it will burn.

I am professionally qualified in metallurgy, and from my limited knowledge of the Russian metallurgical industry, it is my understanding that all Russian military equipment such as tanks, trucks, artillery, and guns, etc., are manufactured out of the finest Russian steel even though on a recent visit to Russia, I observed some military hardware of inferior quality. NO! Lignastone is not widely used in the manufacture of military hardware.

The most likely explanation of this verse is that in our modern technologically advanced warfare, most weapons are propelled by several varieties of rocket fuel. Perhaps it is this fuel the Israelis will capture in sufficient quantity to give them a seven-year supply (Ezek. 39:9).

42. Question: The Bible says that Babylon will never be rebuilt. Yet, Revelation 17 and 18 seem to indicate that it will be. Is there a contradiction?

Answer: The prophecy against Babylon is recorded in Isaiah 13. According to God's Word, Babylon would never rise again, and to demonstrate this Jeremiah took a stone and cast it into the river Euphrates, with the divine statement, " 'So will Babylon sink to rise no more because of the disaster I will bring upon her' " (Jer. 51:64).

The prophecy is very clear. NO! It will never be rebuilt. In fact, the entire site is considered cursed by the locals and the Arab population. The Chinese and the Iraq governments were, however, spending many millions of dollars to restore the site as a tourist attraction prior to the Gulf War of 1991. In fact, Saddam Hussein was planning to move his headquarters from Baghdad to Babylon at that time.

Much restoration work has been undertaken. Buildings

such as Nebuchadnezzar's palace and the Ishtar Procession Way have been completed. Work on the Hanging Gardens were to be started just before the outbreak of the Gulf War. To the best of my knowledge, however, there are no local plans to rebuild the city of Babylon for dwelling purposes. In fact such was the destruction of Baghdad during the Gulf War, any massive building in Iraq would, by necessity, be concentrated on its capital city.

What is the meaning of the Babylon in Revelation 17 and 18? In Revelation 17 and 18 we find Babylon pictured in a twofold way. In chapter 17 she is described as a great harlot, contrasted with the pure bride of Christ in chapter 19. The destruction of apostate Babylon prophesied in chapter 17 portrays the end of Babylon in its ecclesiastical sense. This is much more than papal Rome. It is apostate Christendom, a world religion that has betrayed Christianity, and it is interlocked with the pagan, godless governments of the world.

In Revelation 18 we are confronted with Babylon in a political and economic context. Babylon, the great city, represents all of civilization without God. It is the center of frightful corruption (Rev. 18:2-5), and we see this corruption in every aspect of our modern society. But she will be judged and destroyed in just one day (Rev. 18:8).

So we conclude that Babylon is not so much a physical location as it was in days past, but in present day prophecy it represents an evil influence, both religious and commercial, and will continue in the world until the manifestation of the Lord Jesus Christ in power and great glory.

43. Question: Who are the kings of the North, the South, and of the East as detailed in Bible prophecy?

Answer: The kings represent three federations who, led by mass military forces, converge upon the Holy Land during the time of the Great Tribulation.

RUSSIA

1. The king from the North refers to the northern bloc, or Russia and her allies, which will also include Syria. This great enemy will challenge the authority of the Antichrist, who will have made his seven-year covenant with the Jews. Such passages as Ezekiel 38:1-39; Daniel 11:40; and Joel 2:1-27 describe this confederacy. The Gog of Ezekiel's prophecy is Russia.

Israel is under no illusions as to where the real threat lies. In 1968 Moshe Dayan declared: "The next war will not be with the Arabs but with Russia." As time would tell, the Arabs have openly attacked Israel, but behind this continued threat there lies the hidden hand of Russia. Her aim seems to be twofold:

A. A powerful presence in the Mediterranean. It is generally conceded that whoever controls the Mediterranean, controls the civilized world.

B. The control of Middle East oil. It is estimated that more than two-thirds of the world's oil reserves are located in this area. It is fairly certain that if Russia was contemplating an armed conflict with other powers, her most probable first step would be to move into the oil-producing countries and take control. Interesting and significant is the prophecy recorded centuries before, and found in Ezekiel 38:12. Russia says to herself, "I will go up to take a *spoil!*"

Whatever the timing and/or the direction, one thing is certain — at some future period in time Israel will have to face invasion from the north.

2. The king of the South.

> "At the time of the end the king of the South will engage him in battle, and the king of the North will storm out against him with chariots and cavalry and a great fleet of ships. He will invade many countries and sweep through them like a flood" (Dan. 11:40).

It is generally accepted among prophetic scholars that

Russia - N
Egypt - S

the "king of the South" refers to Egypt, inasmuch as this power is referred to as the south of Israel (Dan. 11:5-9,11,14-15,25,29,40). We know from Daniel 11:43 that this king will wield great power and influence at the end time, in confederation with other powers — Arabic and African.

The hostility of Egypt towards Israel dates back to the childhood of Ishmael and Isaac. It continued during the days of Israel's slavery, reaching a climax at the Exodus and the subsequent destruction of the Egyptian army in the Red Sea.

More recently, under the late President Nasser, antagonism increased to such an extent that by 1976 the aim was to drive the Jews from Palestine. But God's hand has been on the Jew ever since nationhood in 1948. He has miraculously intervened on Israel's behalf, repelling Egyptian aggression three times, in 1948, 1956, and 1967.

To understand Daniel 11 correctly is to observe that at some time in the future a "king of the South" will challenge Israel's right to the land of Palestine. Daniel 11 has in mind a protracted span of history, involving struggles between Egypt under the Ptolemaic dynasty and Syria under the Seleucid dynasty, but it is evident that from verse 40 to the end of the chapter we have a prophetic leap alluding to the time of the end of this age. *China, Japan & India EAST*

3. The kings of the East. Once again there is general agreement among prophetic scholars that the kings of the East represent China, Japan, and India, as well as many of the lesser nations of southeast Asia.

The word "east" comes from the Greek, meaning "the rising of the sun." This would seem to have reference to oriental races and nations. When we consider the future gigantic battle that is to take place in the land of Palestine, involving most of the major nations of the world, it would be most unlikely that the Orient with its teeming millions would remain neutral.

What is the mission of the eastern kings?

In the Book of Revelation there is reference to a great

force that will participate in the final world conflict. It is more than likely that this vast army will emanate from the orient.

1. Revelation 9:13-16 — Here we see an army of horsemen numbering 200 million. One-third of the men were slain in the ensuing military engagement. China now boasts membership of its "Red Army" to be almost 200 million.

2. Revelation 16:12-16 — This is a direct reference to the battle of Armageddon. When the sixth vial is poured out upon the world, the great river Euphrates is dried up. Thus we see that the last great barrier, the ancient border between the empires of east and west, will be breached.

A tremendous military force will move towards Palestine for the final world conflict in the Middle East — a conflict between the forces of evil and the army of the Lord (Rev. 19:11-16).

It is most significant that the Chinese have spent huge sums of money in developing a national road system from east to west. The road from China through the Himalayas to Pakistan is completed. The remainder in Iran and Iraq is due for completion by 1999.

It's later than we think!

7

The Second Coming of Jesus Christ

44. Question: The word "Armageddon" is used quite frequently to depict World War III. When and where will this battle take place?

Answer: The word Armageddon comes from the Hebrew which means "Mount Megiddo." The battle, or more correctly, the campaign of Armageddon will not only be fought near the town of Megiddo in the valley of Jezreel, but the whole land of Palestine will be one great blood bath. This battle is also referred to as *"The Battle of the Great Day of God Almighty."*

The Battle of Armageddon and World War III are not one and the same battle.

Ezekiel 38 and 39 describe World War III, which is fought between Israel and a multi-national force under the command of Russia. This battle takes place on the northern mountains of Israel — probably within the region of Mt. Hermon.

Zechariah 14 and Revelation 14, 16, and 19 describe the battle of Armageddon, which is fought near Megiddo in the valley of Jezreel, and more throughout Israel and as far south as Petra in Jordan. These Scriptures also reveal that neither the opponents nor the outcome of the wars are the same. Furthermore, we learn from Ezekiel 39 that there is a seven-year period between these two battles. (Refer to Chart 10, page 137.)

The Campaign of Armageddon: Sequence of Events

Immediately after the Marriage Supper of the Lamb, the doors of heaven swing open and there before the whole world is Christ on a white horse. Jesus is coming, not alone, but with the armies of heaven — the saints to reign on this earth for a thousand years. However, before the millennial reign can commence, judgment must be finalized. The day Jesus Christ comes back to earth is also known as *The Battle of the Great Day of God Almighty.*

It is impossible to predict the exact sequence of all the battles raging in Israel, but the following offers the most logical deduced from Scripture:

1. Christ will first go to Edom (Petra) and soil His garments in a bloody battle, in which He will rescue the Israelites who have been persecuted by Antichrist and his armies (Is. 63:1-6).

2. He will then go to Megiddo located in the valley of Jezreel in the lower Galilee region of Israel. It is here where the great armies of the world are assembled ready to do battle against Christ and His chosen people the Jew. This conflict is really just another stage in the campaign or battle of Armageddon as described in Revelation 16:12-16.

3. The prophet Joel provides a detailed picture of the future judgment of the nations in the valley of Jehoshaphat, which is considered by many Bible scholars to be another name for the Kidron Valley. (Refer to Joel 3.)

4. The final assault takes place on Jerusalem. The Antichrist and his armies will storm the Holy City, which by this time will resemble scenes reminiscent of World War II. This is the last conflict between Satan and Christ until after

the Millennium, and it will find Satan making one fiendish effort to destroy the promised seed. The Antichrist, under Satan's command, will order his armies to destroy the entire city of Jerusalem, but Christ will come to deliver her and rescue a remnant of the Jews at the last moment, as seen in Zechariah 12:1-9.

5. The victory descent on the Mount of Olives.

This will be the most dramatic moment in world history. It is the day when Jesus Christ again sets His feet upon the Mount of Olives. It will be a unique day (Zech. 14). It will be a day of rejoicing for all the people of God. However, for the lost, it will be a day of darkness and great distress (Matt. 24:29). The blood of millions will flow throughout the land of Israel, as high as the horses' bridles, as finally all the evil forces of the Antichrist are laid to rest for ever (Rev. 14:20).

45. Question: Who are the "Armies of Heaven" that come to earth with Christ?

Answer: The armies of heaven as recorded in Revelation 19:14 are also called "Saints" and "holy ones." They are all glorified, perfect people.

In the Book of Jude, verse 14, we read: "Enoch, the seventh from Adam, prophesied about these men: 'See, the Lord is coming with thousands upon thousands of his holy ones.' "

Who are these Holy Ones?

Identification of these holy ones will give us a clue as to who will come back to reign with Jesus Christ and occupy the millennial kingdom on planet earth for 1,000 years.

I believe Scripture indicates *five groups:*

1. Angels.

"For the Son of man is going to come in his Father's glory with his angels, and then he will reward each person according to what he has done" (Matt. 16:27).

2. All believers of the Church Age.

All believers who die prior to the Rapture go directly to heaven but remain in a "soulish state" (Phil. 1:21). They will receive their glorified bodies first, in accordance with 1 Thessalonians 4:16. Then we who are alive at that moment of Christ's calling for His church will be raptured and immediately receive our glorified body (1 Cor. 15:53).

Seven years later, after the Tribulation judgments, Jesus Christ comes back to this earth: "Look, he is coming with the clouds, and every eye will see him, even those who pierced him; and all the peoples of the earth will mourn because of him. So shall it be! Amen" (Rev. 1:7).

The question we must now ask ourselves is, *"What are the clouds?"* Does this verse refer to physical literal white clouds we see in the sky? **No!** The clouds in this verse are the glorified believers clothed in fine linen, bright and clean, which speaks of the righteousness of the saints (Rev. 19:8).

3. Martyred saints.

All those people left behind at the Rapture will have another chance (not a second chance simply because they haven't accepted their first chance as yet) and the opportunity to accept Christ over the final seven years on the earth as it is known today. According to Revelation 7:13-17, during the first half of the Tribulation judgments a great multitude of people are saved through the preaching of the sealed 144,000 Jewish evangelists. Their salvation was purchased through martyrdom.

4. Sealed Jews.

The 144,000 sealed Jewish evangelists spent the first three and one-half years of the Tribulation proclaiming the gospel of the kingdom of Christ. As they were sealed by God, their ministry was not hindered in any way. They were untouchable by the forces of Antichrist. This gospel of the Kingdom that is preached is exactly the same message preached to a lost world today (Gal. 1:8).

These sealed Jews of Revelation 7 are the same group as seen in Revelation 14. They are now seen standing with the Lamb on heavenly Mt. Zion. How did they get there? They were raptured at the mid-Tribulation point and called home to glory. They had fulfilled their God-given calling during these days of judgment.

5. Old Testament saints.

This is a very important group of people who are often neglected when it comes to incorporating them into the multitude of the redeemed.

When an Old Testament saint died, he went to paradise. (Refer to question 10, page 30.) When Christ died upon the cross He went to paradise (Luke 23:43; Eph. 4:8-10). Then when He ascended to His Father, He took with Him all those in paradise. Today the paradise compartment of sheol is empty. The Old Testament saints are in heaven in a soulish state awaiting their glorified bodies.

Immediately after the description of the Tribulation in Daniel 11, the promised deliverance to Israel at the close of the Tribulation is related.

One of the great events to take place in heaven before Jesus Christ returns to earth is the Marriage Supper of the Lamb. Revelation 19:9 says: "Blessed are those who are invited to the wedding supper of the Lamb." Who are the invited guests? Certainly not the Bride (Church) nor the Bridegroom (Christ). The bride and groom are always automatic participants at their wedding. It is the Old Testaments saints (Heb. 12:22-23).

The Marriage Supper of the Lamb is where the unique union of Jews and Gentiles occurs. No longer will glorified people be known as the Church or Old Testament Jews. Everyone will be saints of the most high. Yes, the Old Testament people will be in that group of holy ones returning to commence the honeymoon with the Lord as each and every group now called saints reign with Christ for a thousand years.

46. Question: Recognizing that Jesus Christ could come back at any time, should a person pursue long-range plans such as marriage, buying a home, etc.?

Answer: This is an interesting question and one I know is on the mind of many Christian young people as they grow up in an uncertain and degenerate generation. The correct biblical answer is **YES.**

In the parable of the "pounds," Jesus gives us the clear instruction "Occupy till I come" (Luke 19:13). Now we can interpret the word "occupy" in two different ways: (a) to take possession of; and (b) to keep on doing business.

If a Christian has totally dedicated his or her life to the Lord, then the Holy Spirit will be leading that person in all of his plans for the future. One should not attempt to change the leadership of the Holy Spirit. God is going to bless in whatever one is doing provided the Lord Jesus Christ is in total control. That is, he or she is not only a professor, but is also a possessor.

We should never give up, fold our arms, and just wait for the Lord to come. We might be idle for a long while.

For the young person asking such questions, the answer is that you should plan for the future — education, marriage, home, or whatever. But — always make sure God is in those plans. The Scriptures instruct us to go right on enjoying the life that God has given us, and preparing to enjoy it all the more while we serve Him and look eagerly for Jesus' return.

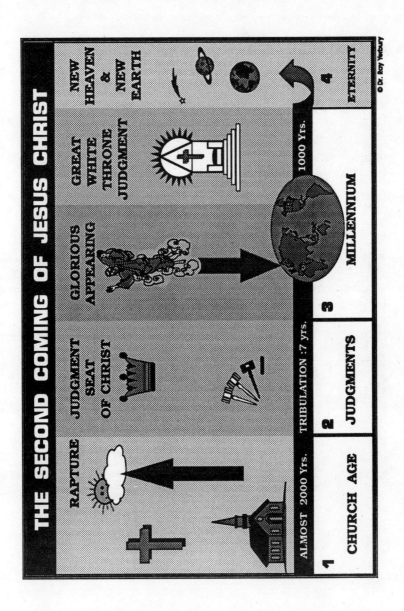

Chart 9. The Second Coming of Jesus Christ

8

The Millennial Kingdom

47. Question: What happens when Jesus Christ returns to earth for the second time?

Answer: The return of Jesus Christ will result in great physical change to the topography of the region in and around the holy city Jerusalem. The Bible says in Micah 4:1: "In the last days the mountain of the Lord's temple will be established as chief among the mountains; it will be raised above the hills, and people will stream to it."

Zechariah 14 is the pinnacle of the apocalypse passages of the Old Testament. This particular passage gives the best description of what will happen on the day Jesus Christ returns to earth to set up His millennial kingdom.

1. The return of Jesus Christ (Zech. 14).

Jesus returns (with His Saints — refer to question 45, page 103) to the Mount of Olives. When His feet touch the earth the mountain will split in two from east to west. A great valley will be formed. That day will be unique in the entire history of the world. The normal weather pattern will be altered. There will be no daytime or nighttime. It would appear that the physical presence of Jesus Christ will obviously provide light so that darkness (the night) cannot prevail.

Living water will now flow out from Jerusalem, half to the eastern Sea (Dead Sea) and half to the western Sea (Mediterranean Sea). Apparently this will be a continuous flow. Today Jerusalem obtains its water from local springs augmented by supplies piped in from the Galilee region.

2. Satan will be "locked and sealed" (Rev. 20:3).

One of the first tasks to be effected is to bind Satan in the abyss, which is done by an ordinary angel. **Why?** "To keep him from deceiving the nations anymore until the thousand years were ended" (Rev. 20:3)

3. There is a "first resurrection" (Rev 20:4-6).

The people who participate in this resurrection are all those who have died as a witness for Christ during the *final* three and one-half years of the Great Tribulation. They will receive their glorified bodies at Christ's coming and will reign with Christ for a thousand years. **Note:** these people now have a glorified body. They do not marry and do not have offspring. (Refer to chart 8, page 91)

4. There is the judgment of the nations (Matt. 25:31-46).

This is also known as the sheep and goats judgment. It would appear from the passage in Daniel 12:11 that this judgment will take 30 days (1290-1260 = 30 days).

The unsaved (goats) go to Hades to wait final judgment at the Great White Throne. The saved of the Tribulation (sheep), those who survived the Tribulation and do not take the "mark of the beast" will enter the millennial kingdom in their fleshly bodies to re-populate the earth under a theocracy — the reign of Jesus Christ for 1,000 years.

What are the extra 45 days in Dan. 12:12 for?

Daniel 12:12 says: "Blessed is the one who waits for and reaches the end of the 1,335 days."

I believe that this will be the time taken to establish Christ's administration for the next 1,000 years — the time to establish lines of communication, receipt of rewards for all the saints, and allocate jobs and positions of authority (refer to Matt 25:14-30 — the parable of the talents).

We must remember that Jesus Christ could establish His administration instantly, without any time delay, if He so willed. However, Jesus is not reigning alone. We are reigning with Him, and even though we will have a more powerful body than we have at present, we will not be all-powerful. We will always have limitations just as the angels have. Apparently it will take this 45 days (1335-1290) to fully set up God's administration on earth.

48. Question: Who will receive rewards, and what will be their purpose?

Answer: For the Christian, the blessed hope or Rapture should be the most thrilling event of the future. However, what most believers fail to realize is that after we receive our glorified bodies (Phil 3:21), when we finally reach heaven and check into those mansions in heavenly glory (John 14:2-3), every believer will stand before Him and give an account of his or her discipleship. This declaration of rewards or loss of rewards (crowns) is called the **judgment seat of Christ.**

How do we receive rewards? Scripture repeatedly mentions **good works!** What does it mean to do good works?

(a) To witness: (Matt. 5:6). To lead a pure life. We as Christians often seem to forget that we are not called upon to be happy, but holy. Holiness is the aim, happiness is the by-product.

(b) To worship: (Matt. 26:7-10). In this story, Jesus referred to worship of himself as good work.

(c) To willingly give: — money, time, talents. Jesus made it abundantly clear that nothing is too small to be considered a good work (Matt. 10:42).

What are *bad works?*

(a) Ones that will not stand the test of fire. They will burn and be revealed as nothing more than wood, hay, and straw (1 Cor. 3:13).

(b) Good works with bad motives (Matt. 6:2).

(c) Our "secret sins" and evil thoughts (1 Cor. 4:5).

(d) Unconfessed sins. This will result in our loss of potential rewards (2 John 8).

Rewards for Christian Service

Crown of life — James 1:12: This is often called the martyr's crown: those who have suffered much for the gospel's sake, and have been "faithful unto death."

Crown of glory — 1 Peter 5:1,4: This is also known as the shepherd's or pastor's crown. A reward for faithful teaching and preaching the Word (Matt. 25:23).

Crown of righteousness — 2 Tim. 4:8: A special crown reserved for all those who have lived a holy life, and are ready and watching for His imminent return.

Crown of rejoicing — 1 Thess. 2:19: This crown is reserved for the soul-winning Christian. Many unsung heroes of faithful witnessing will be rewarded with this crown on that day.

Crown of victory — 1 Cor. 9:25-27: Better known as the incorruptible crown. It will be conferred on all who keep themselves pure from the pleasures of this world.

What is the purpose of crowns? The crowns are symbols of authority. The Queen of England does not need to wear her crown to demonstrate her authority. Neither will we be wearing our crown (that is, if we receive one) to show off to the people of the Millennium how good we might have been in this life. We may be entitled to wear our crown, just as the queen is. However, our immediate purpose is to earn by godly motives our position of service for Christ during the Millennium.

49. Question: Why is the millennial reign of Christ an absolute necessity?

Answer: There are many scholars and Bible teachers who say that the idea of an earthly kingdom is nothing more than a carnal hope. But the Bible knows nothing of a hope for the world, apart from the coming of the Lord who will physically reign on this earth.

I believe there are numerous reasons why there must be a literal reign of Christ on planet Earth. It suffices to mention three major reasons:

1. *The Millennium is necessary to bring about the literal fulfillment of the Old Testament prophecies* — in particular the covenants that God made regarding the ultimate future of Israel. The Word of God is quite clear in Genesis 15:18: "On that day the Lord made a covenant with Abram and said, 'To your descendants I give this land, from the river of Egypt to the great river, the Euphrates.' "

At no time in history has that ever been fulfilled. Even during the great kingdom period under David and Solomon, the nation of Israel never extended its borders to the Euphrates River.

This will and can only eventuate with Christ on the earthly throne. To say there can be no earthly kingdom is to imply that God breaks His word with His earthly people. This comes dangerously close to calling God a liar, and such action is fraught with extreme danger. There must be a literal kingdom if God is to honour His covenants.

We need always to remember that our relationship to Him in the Millennium will be determined by our relationship to Christ in this life as a servant and disciple from the point of salvation to either rapture or death.

2. *The Millennium is necessary to witness the emancipation of creation.* Because of man's sin, the curse of creation will always be on earth (Rom. 8:22). Only when Jesus Christ comes physically to earth again will the curse be lifted on the whole of creation, and that includes animals, plants, and all living matter.

3. *The Millennium will be necessary as a witness to God's delight in His Son.* For more than 30 years God's Son walked this earth, suffered humiliation, and paid the ultimate price with His life. God's answer to this will be full restoration of His Son to a position of exaltation and glory. His kingdom will not be administered by anything or anyone evil, but righteousness will characterize His reign as the supreme sovereign of all the earth.

50. Question: How will people of all nations worship during the Millennium? Will there be churches?

Answer: The passages of Scripture that are most relevant to this question are found in Isaiah 2:2-3:

> In the last days the mountain of the Lord's temple will be established as chief among the mountains; it will be raised above the hills, and all the nations will stream to it. Many peoples will come and say, "Come, let us go up to the mountain of the Lord, to the house of the God of Jacob. He will teach us his ways, so that we will walk in his paths." The law will go out from Zion, the word of the Lord from Jerusalem.

Let us answer the second part of the question first. The tremendous event of salvation began with the Church and will continue through the Tribulation period by the ministry of the 144,000 Jewish evangelists. Even angels will proclaim the same gospel the apostle Paul preached, demonstrating God's infinite mercy even in the midst of judgment. (Rev. 7:1-8; 14:1-5, 6-10).

In fact, entire nations will be saved during the Millennium. But, as we have said before, the Church is not a building, it is God's special people for this age of grace. When the Church is raptured it will cease to function as God intended it to do for this age.

NO! There will not be churches operating as we know them today during the Millennium.

From our Scripture reference, we know that conditions on earth during the Millennium will be entirely different from those of today. After all, Jesus Christ will physically be on earth. Satan will be bound and therefore will have no influence. People will want to worship and those who return to reign with Christ will be the teachers of righteousness to the people who inhabit the Millennium in their fleshly bodies.

How then will people worship?

It is difficult to be dogmatic because the mechanics are not given. Remember, the glorified saints will be God's administrators ensuring His plans for a re-established "Garden of Eden" are carried out.

The nations will not worship in faith, but rather in reality. Today we walk by faith, not by sight. At death, faith becomes reality and we walk by sight in the presence of the glorified Son of God.

The Jews — God's elect will worship in the Lord's temple at Jerusalem. Their worship will not be as in the past — an obedience to the laws of Moses, but rather an acclaiming of the fact that their Messiah-King is dwelling among them.

We also know that the survivors from all the nations that attacked Jerusalem during the Tribulation will now go annually to Jerusalem to celebrate the Feast of Tabernacles (Zech. 14:16). This will be a memorial feast (not sacrificial) to give thanks for the fact of their salvation.

51. Question: Scripture indicates that there will be no more wars during the Millennium! Is this true? If so, how and what will the

nations spend their finances on?

Answer: It is absolutely true that according to Scripture, there is every indication that war will be far from the minds of the Millennium people. It is apparent, however, there will still be disputes among people and nations. The appropriate verse from Scripture is found in Isaiah 2:4:

> He will judge between the nations and will settle disputes for many peoples. They will beat their swords into plowshares and their spears into pruning hooks. Nation will not take up sword against nation, nor will they train for war any more.

This particular verse, or should I say, part of this verse is etched into the base of the stone monument outside the headquarters of the European United Nations building in Brussels, Belgium.

This was the ideal aim of man when the United Nations was established after World War II. However, in reality it has never been achieved. Today more than ever before, wars and disputes affecting most nations of the world are increasing at an alarming rate. Lasting peace will never be achieved while the heart of mankind is filled with evil (Jer. 17:9).

It will only be possible when Jesus Christ comes to reign on planet Earth.

There are a number of other verses relevant to this subject: Isaiah 42:6-7; 54:14-15. The latter is a particular reference to the nation of Israel:

> In righteousness you will be established: Tyranny will be far from you; you will have nothing to fear. Terror will be far removed; it will not come near you. If anyone does attack you, it will not be my doing; whoever attacks you will surrender to you.

What a contrast it will be in the Millennium to that of the current situation within the nation of Israel. Money, peace initiatives, and all the negotiation in the world can and will never buy freedom from terrorism. Only the absence of sin and the binding of its chief perpetrator Satan will achieve that condition.

When we look at the published statistics for a number of today's nations whose country is located in sensitive areas of the world, we observe that in many situations almost 50 percent of the country's budget is allocated to military and social benefits. The obvious question must now be asked: How will those nations spend their money in an ideal environment?

This question is somewhat difficult to answer simply because we are not privy to all that will happen when Jesus Christ becomes the supreme ruler of earth. We can, however, suggest that the allocation of wealth will be evenly distributed. Greed, characteristic of the world today, will be gone, and all people of the world will work in a state of relative harmony.

52. Question: What will conditions be like on the earth during the thousand-year reign of Jesus Christ?

Answer: There are many people who do not believe in a literal Millennium (the thousand-year reign of Jesus Christ on this earth).

One school of thought called amillennialism uses Luke 17:20-21 as their defense and say that the kingdom of God is within you. It is not a literal physical kingdom! And on the surface of this verse it would appear they may be correct. I agree that the kingdom of God is within all of His children, *BUT* it is not consummated until the King comes physically among His people.

This concept is similar to salvation. Salvation is offered as the free gift of God to all who believe (Rom. 6:23). But this salvation is incomplete. It will only be consummated or complete when we meet the Lord and receive our glorified bodies.

Similarly, you cannot have a kingdom without a king, and this we shall see when the King of kings will reign in His physical kingdom on earth for a thousand-year period.

There has to be, and there will be, a physical earthly reign of Jesus Christ. (Refer to question 49, page 113.)

What will conditions on earth be like during the Millennium?

1. Israel will be established in a "Garden of Eden."

What began over 6,000 years ago before sin entered God's creation will once again be established, occupying all that land from the river of Egypt to the Euphrates River (Gen. 15:18).

> On that day the Lord made a covenant with Abram and said, "To your descendants I give this land, from the river of Egypt to the great river, the Euphrates."

This covenant has never been fulfilled and in the light of the current hostilities from the surrounding Arab nations, it would be inconceivable to suggest that such a promise could take place without divine intervention!

2. The physical scene.

At that time when universal peace will be finally established, the land of Israel will, as promised to Moses (Exod. 3:8) be, "a land flowing with milk and honey." It will also be a land where crops will not fail due to bad weather conditions, nor will they be eaten by the locusts as in the past. There will be plenty of grain, wine, and oil for local consumption and probably surplus quantities for export:

> "In that day the mountains will drip with new wine, and the hills will flow with milk; all the ravines of Judah will run with water. A fountain

will flow out of the Lord's house and will water the valley of acacias" (Joel 3:18).

The threshing-floors will be filled with grain; the vats will overflow with new wine and oil. . . . You will have plenty to eat, until you are full, and you will praise the name of the Lord your God, who has worked wonders for you; never again will my people be shamed (Joel 2:24-26).

Famines of greater or lesser intensity have frequently occurred in Palestine because of its dependence upon the rain. Not until modern times has it been possible to store rain in the vast quantities we do today. Famine also occurred naturally when locusts or other insects destroyed the crops. The worst famine named in the Bible occurred in Egypt and the surroundings countries in the time of Joseph (Gen. 41).

During the Millennium, the Scriptures declare that famine will be eliminated.

I will bless them and the places surrounding my hill. I will send down showers in season; there will be showers of blessing. The trees of the field will yield their fruit and the ground will yield its crops; the people will be secure in their land. . . . I will provide a land renowned for its crops, and they will no longer be victims of famine in the land or bear the scorn of the nations (Ezek. 34:26-29).

3. Weather conditions.

Yearly averages of precipitation (rain, melted snow, and other forms of moisture) vary from 4,000 mm in northern Galilee to about 100 mm at the southern tip of the Negev.[7] According to the Bible, rain will come at the appointed time during the Millennium:

Be glad, O people of Zion, rejoice in the Lord your God, for he has given you the autumn rains for righteousness. He sends you abundant showers, both autumn and spring rains, as before (Joel 2:23).

4. Security of tenure is promised.

"The days are coming," declares the Lord, "when the reaper will be overtaken by the plowman and the planter by the one treading grapes. New wine will drip from the mountains and flow from all the hills. I will bring back my exiled people Israel; they will rebuild the ruined cities and live in them. They will plant vineyards and drink their wine; they will make gardens and eat their fruit. I will plant Israel in their own land, never again to be uprooted from the land I have given them" (Amos 9:13-15).

This security of tenure for the Israelites has never been fulfilled until recently, when in 1948 Jews from around the world began to return to their promised land, now under their own administration. Today, it is a partial re-population as suggested by Hosea 3:4-5:

For the Israelites will live for many days without king or prince, without sacrifice or sacred stones, without ephod or idol. Afterwards the Israelites will return and seek the Lord their God and David their king. They will come trembling to the Lord and to his blessings in the last days.

Complete fulfillment of this prophecy will only happen at the conclusion of the seven-year Tribulation period.

5. Evil will be eliminated.

Evil as we know it today will not exist, simply because Satan will be bound and Christ will be in total control reigning from Jerusalem.

He will judge between many peoples and will

settle disputes for strong nations far and wide (Mic. 4:3).

But about the Son he says, "Your throne, O God, will last for ever and ever, and righteousness will be the scepter of your kingdom" (Heb. 1:8).

6. The environment — people and animals.

The Scriptures give a very clear picture as to what the environment will be like during the Millennium:

"But be glad and rejoice for ever in what I will create, for I will create Jerusalem to be a delight and its people a joy. I will rejoice over Jerusalem and take delight in my people; the sound of weeping and of crying will be heard in it no more. Never again will there be in it an infant that lives but a few days, or an old man who does not live out his years; he who dies at a hundred will be thought a mere youth; he who fails to reach a hundred will be considered accursed. They will build houses and dwell in them; they will plant vineyards and eat their fruit. No longer will they build houses and others live in them, or plant and others eat. For as the days of a tree, so will be the days of my people; my chosen ones will long enjoy the works of their hands. They will not toil in vain or bear children doomed to misfortune; for they will be a people blessed by the Lord, they and their descendants with them. Before they call I will answer; while they are still speaking I will hear. The wolf and the lamb will feed together, and the lion will eat straw like the ox, but dust will be the serpent's food. They will neither harm nor destroy on all my holy mountain," says the Lord (Isa. 65:18-25).

No doubt you would have observed that the majority of

the Bible references quoted directly relate to the nation of Israel. Immediately the question arises: What will the conditions be like for the rest of the world?

World conditions during the Millennium

We cannot be absolutely positive in predicting what may happen in other countries. However, we can be reasonably certain that Israel will take the initiative and be the model for the rest of the world to follow. It will be the "super-power" of the Millennium. After all, the headquarters of the Kingdom will be located in Jerusalem.

Psalm 72 gives us the best picture of the millennial reign of Jesus Christ and His relationship to the rest of the world:

> In his day the righteous will flourish; prosperity will abound till the moon is no more. He will rule from sea to sea and from the River to the ends of the earth.... All kings will bow down to him and all nations will serve him.... May his name endure for ever; may it continue as long as the sun. All nations will be blessed through him, and they will call him blessed. Praise be to the Lord God, the God of Israel, who alone does marvellous deeds. Praise be to his glorious name for ever; may the whole earth be filled with his glory. Amen and Amen (Ps. 72:7-8, 11, 17-19).

Characteristics and Nature of the Millennium

1. Peace — Isaiah 2:4; 11:6-9; 65:21; Hosea 2:18; Micah 4:2-5; Zechariah 9:10.

2. Joy — Isaiah 9:3; 30:29; 65:18; Zephaniah 3:14-17.

3. Holiness — Isaiah 1:26-27; 35:8-10; Zephaniah 3:11.

4. Glory — Isaiah 4:2; 40:3-5.

5. Comfort — Isaiah 12:1-2; 40:1; Jeremiah 31:23-25.

6. Justice — Isaiah 9:6-7; Jeremiah 30:9; Ezekiel

34:23; Hosea 3:5; Isaiah 32:16.

7. Complete knowledge — Isaiah 11:9; 54:13; Habakkuk 2:14.

8. Instruction — Isaiah 2:2-3; Micah 4:1-3; Jeremiah 3:14-15.

9. Removal of the curse — Isaiah 11:6-9; 65:25.

10. Sickness removed — Isaiah 33:24; 35:5-7; Zephaniah 3:19.

11. Freedom from oppression — Isaiah 14:3-7; Amos 9:15; Zechariah 9:8; 14:10-11.

12. Longevity will be restored — Isaiah 65:20.

13. Reproduction by human saints — Isaiah 65:23; Ezekiel 47:21-22; Zechariah 10:8.

14. Labor will not be a wasted effort — Isaiah 62:8-9; 65:21-23; Ezekiel 48:18-19.

15. Economic prosperity — Isaiah 30:23-25; 35:1-7; Amos 9:13-15; Joel 2:21-27.

16. Increase in light — Isaiah 4:5-6; 30:26; 60:19-20; Zechariah 2:5.

17. Unified language — Zephaniah 3:9.

18. Unified worship — Isaiah 52:1,7-10; Malachi 1:11; Zechariah 8:23; 14:16.

19. Manifest presence of God — Ezekiel 37:26-28; Zechariah 2:10-13.

20. Palestine will be enlarged — Isaiah 26:15; Obadiah 1:17-21; Genesis 15:18.

21. Land features will change — Zechariah 14:4,8,10 Isaiah 2:2; Ezekiel 47:8-12.

22. Jerusalem will become the worship center of the world — Micah 4:1.

23. Jerusalem renamed — It will be known as "Hephzibah" (Isa. 62:4). The city will be 9.6 kms. in circumference — Ezekiel 48:35.

24. It will have a temple — Isaiah 2:3; Ezekiel 40-48; Joel 3:18; Haggai 2:7-9.

**53. Question: There are many people today say-
ing that by a program of global evange-
lism coupled with social action, the world
can be Christianized and a kingdom established into which Jesus Christ will return. Is this true?**

Answer: This approach to the prophetic Scriptures is
nothing more than "mutton dressed up as lamb," for it was
the commonly held view of eschatology in the Dark Ages.
Indeed, a number of the reformers were perspective enough
to see the folly of such a misguided view.

Martin Luther denounced as false the view that in the
latter days the whole world would turn to Christianity. John
Knox, who was Scotland's greatest reformer, made a scath-
ing attack on such ideas when he said, "The whole earth
never was, nor yet shall be, reformed until the righteous
King and Judge shall appear for the restoration of all
things."[8]

In spite of such condemnation, however, this erroneous
concept persisted and was to a somewhat greater degree
stimulated for a time during the period of the Wesleyan
revivals of the eighteenth century. The great forward thrust
and missionary drive of the Church during the nineteenth
and twentieth centuries gave further stimulus to this school
of thought. However, the onset of two bloody global wars
has served to discredit the theory of a Christianized world.
Now, over recent years, a new or revived school of thought
called the "Christian Reconstruction movement," or "Kingdom Now," has emerged as a significant force to be a danger
in leading believers away from the truth of the gospel.

It is important to ask, "What is the **truth of the gospel**
that makes this misguided teaching a danger?"

1. If the kingdom of God can be established on earth by
means of man's efforts, then there is really no need for Jesus
to come! In his book *The Lord's Return,* William Graham

Scroggie pertinently points out: "If by any process of evolution, or civilization, or promulgation of Christian principles, the world could be brought into the moral and spiritual state we associate with the idea of a Millennium, there would seem to be no need for Christ to come! What makes His return absolutely necessary, if a Kingdom of righteousness is to be established on the earth, is the obvious fact that man is utterly unable to establish such a Kingdom."[9]

2. The Lord's Prayer contains a petition: "Thy Kingdom Come." Now the verb **"come,"** used by the greatest of all teachers, suggests the consummation of the Kingdom at one specific point of time, involving the personal appearance of the King . The verb does not allow for the interpretation that the Kingdom will come by some gradual process initiated by mankind!

3. The word of God is TRUTH (John 17:17). The truth of Scripture repeats itself from generation to generation. In the days of the Judges, the Bible says on no less than four occasions: "In those days Israel had no king; everyone did as he saw fit" (Judg. 21:25). That spirit of anarchy fostered an attitude of apathy, resulting in six of the tribes of Israel failing to carry out God's command to "drive out" the idolatrous inhabitants of Canaan as detailed in Judges 1. Consequently, the situation deteriorated to a state of apostasy, with the Israelites worshipping the idols of Canaan.

This situation which occurred over 3,000 years ago is indicative of conditions in the world and to a large degree in the churches today. When God offered His Son to mankind at His first advent, the response was: " 'We don't want this man to be our king' " (Luke 19:14).

Now, returning to the original question. **NO!** It is not true that mankind through his efforts is to prepare the Kingdom for Jesus Christ to come. It is true, however, that the faithful preaching of the gospel is reaping dividends for the kingdom of heaven. On the other hand, it is also having its setbacks through the activity of Satan and his demons.

The nations of the world have turned their backs on God in response to the devil's gift-wrapped packages of materialism and leisure. The false religions of the world boast of unprecedented advancements across the globe. At the current rate of decay, only the physical return of the Creator will bring about a Kingdom of peace and righteousness as documented in the Scriptures.

54. Question: Why must Satan be released after the thousand-year reign of Christ on this earth?

Answer: The reference to this final revolt at the close of the millennial reign of Christ on earth is found in Revelation 20:7-10:

> When the thousand years are over, Satan will be released from his prison and will go out to deceive the nations in the four corners of the earth — Gog and Magog — to gather them for battle. In number they are like the sands on the seashore. They marched across the breadth of the earth and surrounded the camp of God's people, the city he loves. But fire came down from heaven and devoured them. And the devil, who deceived them, was thrown into the lake of burning sulphur, where the beast and the false prophet had been thrown. They will be tormented day and night for ever and ever.

These verses show that the Millennium will terminate with the release of Satan for a brief period. This will be the concluding test for the world and will result finally in mankind's release from satanic enslavement which began in the Garden of Eden.

We also note that no sooner is Satan released than he resumes his iniquitous activities. He shows that he will not change even after 1,000 years of confinement. In a similar manner, the human response is little better. After an extended period of universal peace and blessing, there is still latent in the human heart an innate evil which is ready to revolt against earth's rightful King, a King who has been amongst His people for 1,000 years.

Not all people will agree with this literal approach. The amillennialist will treat the passage as allegorical, suggesting that Satan's binding (Rev. 20:1-3) is synonymous with Matthew 12:26-29 — that is, the triumphant work of the Cross. Again, according to the amillennial system of reckoning, the thousand years is an extended period between the first and second advents of Christ.

But the fact of Satan's release is clear from Scripture, and the question that nags at our inquiring minds is this: Why man's archenemy should be set at liberty after a long and glorious millennium of righteousness?

I believe there are TWO significant reasons:

1. Mankind will inherit the millennial Kingdom in his fleshly body. Remember, these are the people who have survived the Great Tribulation — the "sheep" from the judgment of the nations. These people will reproduce and have children to re-populate the earth in an ideal environment.

But, even though Satan will be bound and therefore will have no direct influence, mankind in the flesh (those who enter having survived the Tribulation) remains incurably sinful even under the most favorable conditions. What the prophet Jeremiah said about man's nature is characteristic of this age and will be so in the millennial age "The heart is deceitful above all things, and beyond cure" (Jer. 17:9).

Professor Walvoord in his book on Revelation quotes Benjamin Atkinsen as suggesting that "infants born during the Millennium will live to the conclusion of the Millennium and will not be required to make a choice between the devil and Christ until the end."[10] Outwardly there will be conformity to the reign of Christ during the Millennium, but for many, inward reality will be missing. It will be demonstrated beyond question that man, irrespective of his advantages and circumstances, apart from saving grace and the new life of Christ, remains hostile to God.

2. The release of Satan reveals that the Millennium will be necessary to provide a final test for fallen humanity. Walter Scott, in his book *Exposition of the Revelation of Jesus Christ,* comments: "Man has been tried and tested under every possible condition, in every possible way — under goodness, government, law, grace, and now under glory." Even when subjected to a testing under the glorious reign of Christ, man proves a dismal failure. This test at the close of the Millennium will prove this point conclusively.[11]

We see again the wonderful grace of God when this last satanic rebellion will be short-lived, perhaps once again for a seven-year period, but we are not told. Satan will be cast into the lake of fire to join the beast and the false prophet who will precede him by a thousand years.

But, even though Satan will be bound and therefore will have no direct influence, mankind in the flesh (those who enter having survived the Tribulation) remains incurably sinful even under the most favorable conditions. What the prophet Jeremiah said about man's nature is characteristic of this age and will be so in the millennial age: "The heart is deceitful above all things, and beyond cure" (Jer. 17:9).

9

The Eternal Kingdom

55. Question: What is the difference between the millennial reign of Christ and the eternal reign of the Father?

Answer: The millennial reign of Christ will be God's answer to that period of righteousness originally planned at creation: God's Son, Jesus Christ, will reign on this earth as we know it today, although it will be somewhat altered because of the Tribulation judgments.

This Millennium will also be the fulfillment of all that man has sought — perfect government, equity, economic prosperity, and deliverance from greed, pride, insecurity, and fears, all of which plague the modern world. The Millennium will also see the banishment of Satan the devil. He will be rendered powerless, bound and despatched to the abyss at the commencement of the thousand years and there he will stay for its duration. What a prospect — a world without a devil! This will be the promised "stone kingdom" of Daniel 2:44, which will break into pieces earthly kingdoms and become a universal dominion.

The eternal reign of the Father is the ultimate glorious prospect of all believers. It will be the age of glory, when righteousness will not merely reign on a patched up earth, but will dwell in the new or renewed heavens and earth.

It is important to understand at this juncture that, after the Millennium, Christ's reign does not cease. Rather it will extend and unite with the eternal kingdom of God the Father, our blessed Lord and Saviour.

The Church Age is the period of Christ's concealed glory.

The Millennial Age will be the period of Christ's revealed glory.

The Eternal Age will be the period of the Father's sovereignty when Christ delivers His rule to the Father and becomes himself subject to the Father, so that God may be all in all (1 Cor. 15:24-28).

56. Question: Who will be judged before the Great White Throne?

Answer: The Great White Throne judgment represents the last and final judgment for all the unsaved sinners. Every one from Adam and Eve to the present who rejected firstly the Law then secondly Jesus Christ, will attend this judgment. (Refer to chart 5, page 54.)

One day the apostle Paul was invited by the intellectuals of Athens to explain the doctrines he had been preaching. This is part of what he had to say on Mars Hill:

> "In the past God overlooked such ignorance, but now he commands all people everywhere to repent. For he has set a day when he will judge the world with justice by the man he has appointed. He has given proof of this to all men by raising him from the dead" (Acts 17:30-31).

There are a number of important points that arise from that Bible passage:

1. When will this judgment take place?

After the Gog and Magog battle at the end of the Millennium, just prior to the ushering in of the eternal reign of the Father in the new heavens and new earth (Rev. 20:11).

There is a definite date on the divine calendar to which every sinner has an appointment and one to which he must and will keep. There can be no excuses. The unrepentant sinner will stand before God on that appointed day. The picture of the Great White Throne and the horror of the scene is formidable.

2. By what standard will the sinner be judged?

By the law of God which demands perfection (James 2:10). The ultimate standard of course is the man Jesus Christ — the perfect sinless Son of God. He was always obedient to His Father's will. God as our Heavenly Father demands perfection and our lives are measured "by that man whom He has ordained."

3. What is the charge?

Every unbeliever will face judgment for every sin committed. God's Divine diaries will be opened, and every sin committed by every sinner in word, thought or deed, will be judged.

> And I saw the dead, great and small, standing before the throne, and books were opened. Another book was opened, which is the book of life. The dead were judged according to what they had done as recorded in the books. The sea gave up the dead that were in it, and death and Hades gave up the dead that were in them, and each person was judged according to what he had done (Rev. 20:12-13).

This is a judgment unto eternal death. When the "book of life" is opened and their names are not found, they will then be judged out of the "book of man's works." Thus the vital issue on judgment day as the unbeliever stands before Almighty God at the Great White Throne is the fact that he has rejected the Saviour and His plan of salvation through the Cross.

4. What will be the verdict?

The answer is simple: **GUILTY!** His destiny is not some place where reformation can take place. It will not be a huge compound where all the "baddies" can have a good time as some would like to suggest. **NO!** The Bible is very clear as to the sinner's destiny:

> If anyone's name was not found written in the book of life, he was thrown into the lake of fire (Rev. 20:15).

Hell is isolation forever and ever. God has done everything possible to save the sinner from hell. But God is holy and must punish the sinner.

57. Question: What is the difference between the throne of Revelation 4, and the throne of Revelation 20?

Answer: The central object in heaven is the throne of God, referred to eight times in the first six verses of chapter 4, and a total of 18 times in chapters 4 and 5. This will be the most glorious sight that greets the believer when he is ushered into the presence of Jesus Christ by an angel at death, or, after the Rapture, is taken into the throne room as a united group of the redeemed.

This throne would appear to be the focal point in heaven, with everything else located in relationship to it. Such expressions as, "about the throne," "in the midst of the throne," and "before the throne" support this idea.

What other features of the throne in heaven do we learn from Revelation 4?

1. The triune God (John says "one who sat there") was on the throne (verses 2-3).

2. Twenty-four thrones surround the central throne

with 24 elders seated upon them (verse 4).

3. There are signs of the coming judgment (lightning and thunderclaps) proceeding out of the throne (verse 5).

4. The seven spirits of God are before the throne. The sevenfold characteristics of the Holy Spirit are revealed in Isaiah 11:2: The Spirit of the Lord, wisdom, understanding, council, might, knowledge, fear of the Lord.

5. Before the throne there is "a sea of glass, clear as crystal." Although one cannot be dogmatic as to the meaning of the sea of glass, I tend to believe it to be the Church at rest, untroubled by the winds and storms of earthly life (verse 6).

6. There are four living creatures before the throne. They are seraphim, described by Isaiah in his vision of the throne of God (Isa. 6:1-3) (verses 6-9).

7. There is heavenly worship of the Lord Jesus Christ by the living creatures and the 24 elders before the throne (verses 8-11). These verses, together with those in chapter 5 describe the fact that the Lord Jesus Christ is the object of worship in heaven.

The Great White Throne of chapter 20 is the exclusive judgment throne for all the sinners who have rejected salvation. It would appear that the only time this throne is used is for the final judgment after the Millennium but before the eternal Kingdom. (Refer also to question 56, page 130.)

58. Question: Why is it necessary for planet Earth to be destroyed? Why can't we live on earth with Jesus Christ reigning forever?

Answer: The appropriate verses of Scripture relative to the destruction of this earth are:

> But the day of the Lord will come like a thief. The heavens will disappear with a roar; the elements will be destroyed by fire, and the earth and

everything in it will be laid bare (2 Pet. 3:10).

"Behold, I will create new heavens and a new earth. The former things will not be remembered, nor will they come to mind" (Isa. 65:17).

Then I saw a new heaven and a new earth, for the first heaven and the first earth had passed away, and there was no longer any sea (Rev. 21:1).

Planet Earth must be destroyed and this is simply because it is contaminated with sin. Even though the earth will be relatively free of sin (as we know sin today) during the millennial reign of Jesus Christ, the earth will still be tainted with sin from the past, and by that brief period when Satan is released at the end of the Millennium.

The ultimate plan has always been for mankind to live with the Father, whose heavenly Jerusalem will come down to earth (Rev. 21:2). God cannot look upon any sin. That is why He forsook His Son for three hours while on the cross (Mark 15:34). God could not even contemplate a visit to this contaminated earth. It has to be destroyed and a new earth created for God to dwell amongst His people.

The heavens must also be destroyed. Unseen to our vision, there is in the heavenly realm a great spiritual battle raging between the forces of God's angels and Satan's demonic forces. The present heavens (not the third heaven where God dwells — 2 Cor. 12:2) are the dwelling place of the forces of Satan and the fallen angels who are still free. It is therefore contaminated, and is totally unsuitable for the future dwelling place of the redeemed.

59. Question: Are we given any information in the Bible about God's city called the "New Jerusalem"?

Answer: Yes! In the Book of Revelation, chapters 21 and 22, we are provided with sufficient information to thrill our hearts and to excite us beyond our wildest imagination. Within these chapters there are many new concepts which, with our limited understanding we find difficult to explain. Basically, there are five new concepts:

1. The new Jerusalem. This is the Holy City, heavenly Mt. Zion, a city in the sky, the dwelling place of God, and is described as a 1,500 mile (2,400 kms) cube. Its walls are pure gold; its foundations are of pure stones; its streets are transparent. More importantly, this city has no temple. The city has no light bearers. The very presence of God within gives it light. "The nations will walk by its light, and the kings of the earth will bring their splendour into it" (Rev. 21:24).

2. There is a new heaven and a new earth. We considered this particular concept in the previous question. It is important to understand that there are three heavens:

(a) The atmospheric heaven around the earth;

(b) Stellar heaven containing the galaxies;

(c) The third heaven, or the throne of God.

It is the atmospheric heaven which is the abode of Satan (Eph. 6:12; Job 1:7). This part of the heavens is contaminated with evil, and will be destroyed to make way for the new heavens together with the new earth.

The Holy City, which our Lord went to prepare for His saints (John 14:1-3), will come down from heaven to this new earth. No longer will God's tabernacle be in the third heaven. He will move His headquarters to the new earth (the saints' eternal new home), and will take up His abode in the New Jerusalem.

3. There will be a new Paradise. The apostle John paints a picture of the water of life. Its clear water flows from the throne of God right through the center of the city. The trees by the bank yield fruit: its leaves are for the "healing of the nations." There is no curse and no darkness, all of which are a product of sin. There will be personal access to God, and we will reign for ever and ever (Rev. 22:5).

4. There is a new form of humanity

Very little detail is revealed about life in our new surroundings. We do know, however, that nations and kings still exist. Angels will be present and will co-exist with human saints. The scene is certainly far removed from our present weak situation. Our new bodies will be characterized by power and controlled by the spiritual rather than subject to the physical.

Perhaps the scene in the upper room may give us a small clue. Christ appeared to His disciples through a locked room. He ate with them. On another occasion He cooked their breakfast beside the Sea of Galilee (John 21). He was uniquely flesh, without blood. Jesus himself said to His disciples, " 'Touch me and see; a ghost does not have flesh and bones, as you see I have' " (Luke 24:39). The apostle Paul said, "I declare to you brothers that flesh and blood cannot inherit the kingdom of God" (1 Cor. 15:50). Yes, Jesus was uniquely flesh and bone. He was also totally recognizable, but yet was different, and one day we will be like Him (1 John 3:2). What an expectation!

5. We will have a new vocation. In the beginning God created not a static but a dynamic world. He created the Garden of Eden, then further created Adam and Eve to share in His creation. Did God then say, "Sit back Adam and Eve. Relax and enjoy life"? **No!** Adam was told to work and take care of the garden (Gen. 2:15).

Does God work or does He just sit back on a throne and direct the affairs of the universe? No! I believe the Bible is quite clear as to the activity of the Godhead. John 5:17 says: "Jesus said to them, 'My Father is always at his work to this very day, and I, too, am working.' "

Now we are not told what God has in mind for us in our new dwelling on a newly created or recreated earth, but you can be sure that such an active and creative God would not shape eternity for a passive existence.

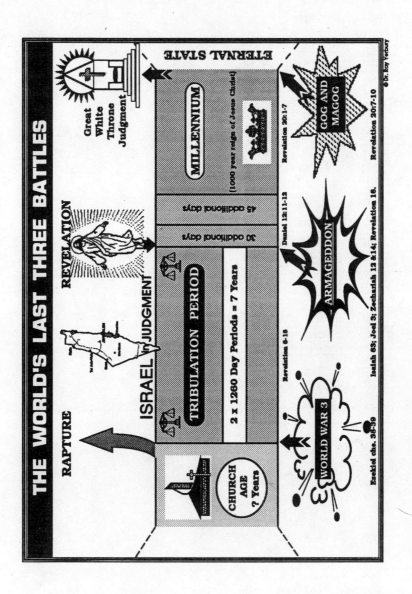

Chart 10. The World's Last Three Battles

10
Current Prophetic Issues

60. Question: What are some of the signs we see in the world today that indicate Christ's imminent return?

Answer: There are many signs that clearly point to the imminent return of Jesus Christ. The clearest sign is the establishment of the modern state of Israel in 1948.[12]

We have a number of general signs such as wars, famine, and earthquakes, that point to Christ's return. But today we see other vital signs in the world and they are all confirmed by Scripture.

Six Major Signs

1. Knowledge and travel. The Bible says in Daniel 12:4: "But you, Daniel, close up and seal the words of the scroll until the time of the end. Many will go here and there to increase knowledge."

Poor old Daniel didn't have a clue what this meant, and neither did our grandparents. It has all happened over the past 20 years. Never before has the world placed so much emphasis on education and traveling to all parts of the globe to obtain it; and it is not only the businesses, government, and the educational institutions who are traveling and learning; the church is now in on the act.

Today we have seminars, conferences, pastor's retreats, congresses, and meetings for every conceivable type of activity known to man. We travel thousands of miles to get there and money seems no object.

What about **leisure?** The travel industry is booming. I think the world has finally arrived at the point where people today are delighted to be identified with a *"leisure/pleasure-seeking, fun-hungry, money-grabbing, God-rejecting, I'll-do-it-my-way society.* And God is saying, "Very well — go ahead. BUT! One day you will give an account of all that you have done."

2. Violence. We see today an alarming social deterioration. We live in a violent society. A decade ago Australian cities were comparatively safe. But not today! There has been an alarming increase in such violent crimes as rape, murder, armed robbery, street bashings, and home break-ins with incredible violence.

In January 1989 the Australian Institute of Criminology called on the media to "present a more accurate and less violent view of Australian society" — and what happened? A few hours later, the assistant commissioner of the Australian Federal Police was brutally murdered outside his Canberra home. No one is safe on the streets at night. Police officers appear to be prime targets. Late night trains are downright dangerous and no one country is isolated from this form of violence. BUT, it is not only in the streets; it's now no longer safe in the home. Fear is written across the face of thousands of women — and you gauge the level to which society has fallen when you take note of the multitude of women living in *"defacto relationships."* And there is child abuse, child abduction — the list is endless.

What does the prophetic word have to say about all this?

Do not be deceived: God is not mocked. A man reaps what he sows. The one who sows to please his sinful nature, from that nature will reap destruction; the one who sows to please the Spirit, from the Spirit will reap eternal life (Gal. 6:7-8).

Sodom and Gomorrah and the surrounding towns gave themselves up to sexual immorality and perversion (Jude 7).

Now the men of Sodom were wicked and were sinning greatly against the Lord (Gen. 13:13).

The Lord saw how great man's wickedness on the earth had become, and that every inclination of the thoughts of his heart was only evil all the time. . . . Now the earth was corrupt in God's sight and was full of violence (Gen. 6:5,11).

But the Lord also had something to say about the future. We are told in Luke 17:26, " 'Just as it was in the days of Noah, so also will it be in the days of the Son of Man.' "

Now the Bible distinctly tells us that men were taken up entirely with eating, drinking, marrying, buying, selling, planting, and building. There is nothing wrong with all of these except what the Word of God is saying here is that they attended to nothing else. They were totally pre-occupied with the world and did not need Christ . . . and what happened? The Flood came at last in Noah's day and drowned all except those who were in the ark. The fire fell from heaven at last in Lot's day and destroyed all except Lot, his wife, and his daughters. Then Lot's wife was disobedient and she too was destroyed.

And our Lord declares that there is going to be an action replay of judgments when He comes again at the end of this age.

3. Community acceptance of homosexuality. The acceptance of homosexuals is not an overnight phenomenon. Without doubt the seeds have been sown in the liberal educational system with very little or no reference to God's moral laws. As a result the harvest has been promiscuity of monumental proportions across the nations of the world.

The Organization for Sexual Equality in Sweden states, "When two applicants for a public job have all other qualifications in common, the homosexual should have priority to the job." It's an added qualification, they say.[13]

What does the Bible say about homosexuality? The irrevocable, eternal law of God makes its position very plain: " 'If a man lies with a man as one lies with a woman, both of them have done what is detestable. They must be put to death; their blood will be on their own heads' " (Lev. 20:13).

Now you may wonder why "capital punishment" was decreed when homosexuality was practiced! The answer is simply because sin beareth sin. Homosexuality is not self-contained or limited to the one practicing it, but rather draws others into this sin of abomination and defiles an entire community or nation.

When the prophet Daniel identified the Antichrist, he revealed one characteristic of this lawless one with the words, "He will show no regard for the gods of his father or for the one desired by women" (Dan. 11:37).

4. The return of the Jews to Israel. Since the late eighties the world has given witness to a large migration of Jews coming back to their homeland from many countries across the globe. The majority of these people have returned [called the *ailyah*] from the old Soviet Russia, or C.I.S. as it is known today. In 1990, approximately 14,000 black Jews known as *"Falasha"* were flown out of Ethiopia to Israel within 24 hours in an exodus known as "Operation Solomon."

There is an air of excitement as the Israeli society is being galvanized into a mighty nation. However, all this activity associated with the movement of Jews back to the land of promise to await their Messiah is in part fulfillment of the prophetic word as spoken by Ezekiel in chapter 20:33-34; and 36:24:

> "As surely as I live, declares the Sovereign Lord, I will rule over you with a mighty hand and an outstretched arm and with outpoured wrath. I will bring you from the nations and gather you from the countries where you have been scattered — with a mighty hand and an outstretched arm and with outpoured wrath.
>
> "For I will take you out of the nations; I will gather you from all the countries and bring you back into your own land."

This prophecy was only partially (if ever) fulfilled in 537-536 B.C. when God's people returned from the captivity in Babylon. Since the days of the captivity in Babylon they have never been in their own land totally, and under their own administration until May 14, 1948.

5. The rise of apostasy in the Church. One of the specific signs of Christ's imminent coming which is more pronounced today than in any prior century is that of apostasy within the so-called Christian church.

The apostle Paul, writing to Timothy, warned in latter times this would happen.

> The Spirit clearly says that in later times some will abandon the faith and follow deceiving spirits and things taught by demons (1 Tim. 4:1).
>
> But mark this: There will be terrible times in the last days. People will be lovers of themselves, lovers of money, boastful, proud, abusive, disobedient to their parents, ungrateful, unholy, without love, unforgiving, slanderous, without self-control, brutal, not lovers of the good, treacherous, rash, conceited, lovers of pleasure rather than lovers of God — having a form of godliness but denying its power. Have nothing to do with them (2 Tim. 3:1-5).

This apostasy is not merely concerned with peripheral issues such as for example the length of the creation day, or the fact and events surrounding the crucifixion; but rather strikes at the core of Christian doctrine. The following list will shock many as to the content of the liberal theologians message in churches today:

* The Word of God is doubted. It is the product of human thought. Qualified inerrancy.
* The deity of Christ is denied. Christ has been declared a good man and prophet.
* The Virgin Birth is questioned. Mary was only engaged to Joseph at the time of conception, therefore Christ was born out of wedlock.
* Jesus Christ had an extra-marital affair with Mary Magdalene.
*The bodily Resurrection is clouded with hypothetical suggestions such as the fraud, swoon, vision, spirit and /or heart theories.
* The promise of Christ's second coming is dismissed as a "pie in the sky" or even a hoax.

One of the characteristics of the Christian church today is the rapid rise in the number of false prophets. While apostasy gives rise to false prophets, strictly speaking there is a difference. Apostasy refers to those who once knew the truth but have turned away in error. One may be a false prophet having no previous knowledge of the truth. So therefore, apostasy is a worse sin.

The apostle Peter when speaking of the apostate preachers said in 2 Peter 2:21-22:

It would have been better for them not to have known the way of righteousness, than to have known it and then to turn their backs on the sacred command that was passed on to them. Of them the proverbs are true: "A dog returns to its vomit," and,

"A sow that is washed goes back to her wallowing
in the mud."

For the APOSTATE condition there can be only one
remedy and that is JUDGMENT.

6. The incessant call for world peace.

I believe we have now entered the most dangerous
period of current world politics — yet humanity does not
realize it, and the Church is oblivious to the times of the
signs.

In the 1960s, President Kennedy and Soviet leader
Khrushchev came together for a summit meeting. The world
hoped for an easing of tension. But, what happened? The
Soviets had the Berlin Wall built.

Toward the end of the seventies, President Carter met
with Soviet leader Brezhnev in Vienna to sign the SALT II
missile treaty. The two exchanged kisses. What was the
result? The Russians marched into Afghanistan. They with-
drew in 1988 after 1.5 million Afghans had lost their lives —
another total failure.

On December 8, 1987, at the Washington Summit,
Soviet party secretary Gorbachev was presented as the
"sunny boy and darling" of the media. In May 1989 the West
Germans hailed him as a hero. The German foreign minister
was the loudest to shout. He said, "This is the first step
towards WORLD PEACE! The threat of war is diminishing
considerably."

In 1993 we witnessed the signing of the P.L.O./Israeli
peace treaty which promised peace for both Palestinians and
Jews. In 1994, at the desert border crossing, Jordan's King
Hussein and Israel's Prime Minister Yitzhak Rabin co-
signed their treaty of friendship within a barbed wire fence
surrounded by a minefield.

Outside this wire-rimmed islet of peace, sounds could
be heard in the north where militiamen, presumably from
the Muslim extremist group Hizballah in Lebanon ex-

changed fire with Israeli troops. And in the Gaza Strip the Palestine Liberation Organization leader Yassir Arafat, with whom Israel made peace in September 1993, called a general strike to protest a clause in the treaty that lends weight to Jordan's claim to protect Jerusalem's Muslim holy places.

What a paradox! In the midst of unprecedented peace calls, the United States and the Russians together spend about $1.5 billion a day on military defense. A number of developing countries spend almost four times as much on arms as they do on health for their people. Yet 20 percent of their children die before their fifth birthday.[14]

While in the Western world one hears much about the progress of world peace, in reality, it is clear there can be no lasting peace. **Why?** Because war is one item on the Lord's agenda specifically mentioned for the end times. "When you hear of wars and revolutions, do not be frightened. These things must happen first, but the end will not come right away" (Luke 21:9). All over the world a master-piece of deception is taking place: **the peace deception.** People have fears or have been made to have fears about everything. People fear certain kinds of food, fish, flour, meat treated with isotopes, the greenhouse effect, the dark, and the list is endless. People fear just about everything except for the *"great and terrible day of the Lord"* — that promised day Jesus said would come totally unexpectedly. First Thessalonians 5:3 says:

> While people are saying "Peace and safety," destruction will come on them suddenly, as labour pains on a pregnant woman, and they will not escape.

61. Question: Who is the madman from Russia who would be Gog?

Answer: Never before has an apparently obscure figure in world politics risen to a position of influential power in such a short period of time. In the December 1993 free elections held in Russia, Zhirinovsky's Liberal-Democratic party (LDP) won 24 percent of the popular vote. So then, who is Vladimir Volfovich Zhirinovsky? Who is the man who arrogantly claims that he will be the next president of Russia in 1996? Here are seven terrible facts about this rising star of Russia — this populist demagogue who has pledged to restore his nation's glory — and its empire — even at the risk of war.

Vladimir Zhirinovsky: The madman who would rule Russia

1. His given name is "Vladimir," which means "master of the world." His middle name of "Volfovitch" indicates his father was a wild canine, and his recent but continual wild statements reveal an evil and ambition unknown in the animal kingdom.

2. Many in Russia claim that his father was Jewish. Records in the government archives in Alma-Ata, the capital of the largely Muslim central Asian republic of Kazakhstan, where he was born, supports this claim. Although he will deny it, the man known today for outspoken anti-Semitism was born Vladimir Volfovitch Eidelshtein. His biological father Volf Isakovich Eidelshtein was Jewish. Vladimir's mother was married previously to Andrei Vasilyevitch Zhirinovksy, but he had died 20 months before baby Vladimir was born.

He is well known for his strong anti-Semitic statements, blaming the Jews for the first two world wars. Furthermore, he has stated that *when* (not if) he comes to power, he will not tolerate two million Jews governing a country of some 190 million Russians.

3. He has uttered a myriad of outrageous statements and threats. He threatened World War III when Germany refused to let him visit that country. He recently said, "Let us make others suffer." And concerning Lithuania he said, "I'll

bury radioactive waste along the Lithuanian border and put up powerful fans and blow the stuff across at night. They'll all get radiation sickness. They'll die of it. When they either die or get down on their knees, I'll stop."[15]

4. There are strong rumors circulating that he is a homosexual.

5. He is being compared to Adolph Hitler. He is strongly supported by the Russian military. This is understandable when you consider the outlandish promises his party made in the December 12, 1993, parliamentary elections. Will he be able to give every retiree from the armed services a free home on the Baltic Sea? Unlikely in a land experiencing economic chaos and hyper-inflation!

6. He is an ultra-nationalist who desires to recreate the Russian Empire and abrogate the 1867 treaty deeding Alaska to the United States of America. His grand plan includes the annexation or control of wide sections of Poland, Finland, Afghanistan, Turkey, Iran, and the Baltic States.

7. His ultimate statement was made in a recent television interview when he said that invasion of the Persian Gulf was a possibility. In fact, he advocates Russian conquest and control of the Persian Gulf and the Mediterranean. The title of his autobiography is *Last Thrust to the South*.

The Word of God in Ezekiel 37 and 38 declares that in the end time a power-crazed ruler referred to as **"GOG"** will come down on Israel from the north — a massive Russian-Islamic invasion. Other countries including Germany, Turkey, Iran (ancient Persia), Sudan, Lybia, and Ethiopia will join forces with Russia for the express purpose to annihilate the Jew.

While we cannot be emphatic that this man is the Gog of Ezekiel (not a real name but a title similar to a Czar or Kaiser), he certainly exhibits many of the characteristics that such a leader will undoubtedly possess. Zhirinovsky himself may disappear into the background, but the forces of discontent he represents won't disappear.

We should keep our eyes on this man or other members of his political party, together with the nation of Israel in the coming days.

More importantly, however, we should take heed of Luke's instruction: "When these things begin to take place, stand up and lift up your heads, because your redemption is drawing near" (Luke 21:28).

62. Question: Will Russia invade Israel?

Answer: In summary, **YES.**

The Scriptures are quite clear as to the fact that at the end time the nation of Russia and its allies will invade the land of Palestine. But there is another fact that is also certain, and it is that when Russia strikes Israel, God will strike Russia, for Israel is the "apple of His eye" (Zech. 2:8).

Nowhere in all of the Scriptures do we find a declaration of divine opposition to a specific nation, which is more direct and definite than God's avowed wrath towards Russia.

Ezekiel 39:1-5 is a prophecy directly against this northern power. This is what the sovereign Lord says:

"I am against you, O Gog, chief prince of Meshech and Tubal. I will turn you around and drag you along. [The Kings James Version says, "I will turn thee back, and leave but the sixth part of thee."] I will bring you from the far north and send you against the mountains of Israel. Then I will strike your bow from your left hand and make your arrows drop from your right hand. On the mountains of Israel you will fall, you and all your troops and the nations with you. I will give you as food to all kinds of carrion [ravenous] birds and to the wild animals. You will fall in the open field, for I have spoken, declares the Sovereign Lord."

The prediction of the destruction of the Russian defense

forces could hardly be more clearly enunciated. However, Ezekiel's prophecy in chapter 39 continues its vivid description of the carnage:

> "On that day I will give Gog a burial place in Israel, in the valley of those who travel east towards the Sea. It will block the way of travellers, because Gog and all his hordes will be buried there. . . . For seven months the house of Israel will be burying them in order to cleanse the land. All the people of the land will bury them, and the day I am glorified will be a memorable day for them, declares the Sovereign Lord (Ezek. 39:11-13).

This same prophecy reveals that it will take **seven years** to burn all the fuel and weapons belonging to the multinational forces under the command of the Russian army. This gives us a clue as to when this battle might take place. It is unlikely that such a mammoth clean-up operation would take place after the return of Christ. We can therefore safely predict that this battle in the northern hills of Israel will occur just prior to, or at the commencement of the great Tribulation.

This battle with Russia and its allies must take place approximately seven years before the return of Jesus Christ. It is not the battle or campaign of Armageddon. This occurs at the time of Christ's return.

Note: For an explanation of Gog and Magog, refer to question 40 on page 93.

63. Question: Recent reports indicate that the Euphrates River is drying up! Is this significant in terms of end-time prophecy?

Answer: The report is correct. The mighty Euphrates River has in fact been drying up for a number of years.

When the lights go out in Damascus and other major cities throughout Syria; when elevators are stuck and even the expensive videos in the luxury hotels cease to function — people grumble and complain but generally accept these power failures as a way of life.

I experienced a similar situation just recently in central India where they are in the grip of a significant drought.

Hospitals and government facilities more often than not run their emergency generators. At all levels of society there is malfunctioning of government and industry under the leadership of the current dictator Hafez Assad.

Why is the power failing?

It is due to the failure of Syria's Russian-built hydro-electric plants on the Euphrates River. Years ago German experts predicted that the water supply would grow dangerously low and today it has become a reality.

The mighty Euphrates River rises in the mountains of eastern Turkey where the authorities have built a number of hydro-power plants. This has caused the water level to drop over 50 percent of normal. As a result, the ecological balance along the upper Euphrates River has been upset. Mudslides have occurred, further reducing the water flow. Today these large hydro-electric power plants which were expected to produce 800 megawatts of power are only producing 250 megawatts.

What does the Bible say about the Euphrates River in end-time prophecy?

> The sixth angel poured out his bowl on the great river Euphrates, and its waters were dried up to prepare the way for the kings from the East (Rev. 16:12).

What is the purpose of the drying up of the Euphrates River? As the Scripture says, "To make way for the kings of the east." Nations such as China, India, Pakistan, Japan, and countries from South-East Asia, guided by the sovereign will of Almighty God, will move across Iran, Iraq, and Syria to assemble in the Valley of Jezreel, to the place that in the

Hebrew is called Armageddon. This great army of 200 million (Rev. 9:16) will come as a response to a call from the Antichrist to plunder Israel, but will meet their judgment in Israel and be annihilated by Jesus Christ at the time of His second coming.

It is important to understand that God is not dependent upon man for the drying up of the Euphrates or any river for that fact. He could do that simple task just as He did at the Red Sea and the Jordan. But what God so often does is to combine the natural with the supernatural, just the way it will happen in the end-time judgments.

64. Question: What is the "New World Order" we hear so much about in our daily newspapers and on television?

Answer: This New World Order comes dressed up in a number of colorful packages such as "Asia's New Age," "A United Europe," "The Age of Aquarius," and by-and-large it identifies closely with the New Age movement.

Irrespective of what name one might attach to this New World Order, I believe it is all part of a worldwide conspiracy — the mystery of Iniquity, "Babylon the Great" of Revelation 18.

At Brussels in May 1989, NATO leaders ended their summit with a challenge to the Soviet bloc to "create a new political order in Europe." They went on to say. "We want to overcome the painful division of Europe, which we have never accepted. We want to move beyond the post-war period . . . we seek to shape a new world order of peace in Europe."

At the United Nations assembly in December 1988, the then leader of the Soviet Republic, Mikhail Gorbachev, called for a New World Order for the twenty-first century. In 1989 we saw where Deng Xiaoping of China reached out for the late Rajiv Gandhi's hand and said, "Welcome my young friend."

Gandhi from India wrote a letter to Benazir Bhutto of Pakistan and said, "You and I are children of the New Age."[16]

Hands are shaking, not only in Asia, but all over the world, even in many of the world trouble spots such as the Middle East.

One of the most convincing arguments in favor of the creation of a one-world government has been that the governments of individual nations are no longer able to deal with the growing number of problems that have become global in scale — such as pollution, acid rain, ozone depletion, and atmospheric abuse. We even see a situation today where there is a pooling of ideas and resources between all countries involved in the space program.

Who would have ever imagined a few years ago seeing USA and Russian astronauts waving to one another in outer space?

The arguments for the necessity of a New World Order are very convincing, certainly to the rational mind. I am not against any genuine effort to solve world problems, but my concern is that man is trying by his own efforts and resources to make a world of peace and prosperity, while at the same time he is totally rejecting the Prince of Peace. While he continues on that futile path to self destruction, his efforts will all be in vain.

I do not believe we are seeing a genuine New World Order, but rather a desperate cosmetic change in the hope of survival in the face of insurmountable national problems. These conditions have all resulted from greed, corruption, pride, and rejecting the moral and spiritual laws of God.

The Word of God is again clear as to the fact that the Lord Jesus Christ is to come back to earth and take charge of the affairs of this world's administration. He will govern in righteousness. This reign of Christ will be far superior to the best of man's noblest governments. The reign of Christ will not merely be a regime of peace, righteousness, and justice. It will be of an altogether different order — not a New World Order, but a **HEAVENLY ORDER.**

65. Question: The New Age movement is saying that Christianity has failed in its mission. Now it is our turn to give the leadership to the world! What implications does this have for the believer?

Answer: The first lie in world history was addressed to the women by the serpent. "Your eyes shall be opened, and you will be like God" (Gen. 3:5). This is the general theme song of the New Age movement.

So what is this New Age movement that is gathering momentum around the world to such a degree that an article published in a South Carolina newspaper — the *Columbia Record* — describes in a full page headline: "New Age Dawns in Colombia. Colombians Welcome This New Demonic Religion."[17]

The New Age network which has its roots firmly planted with the 1960s peace, harmony, and back-to-nature movement, emphasizes spiritual well-being and seeking the truth from within. As with all false teachings or cults, self-redemption is the central core of the doctrine. This new philosophy of thought for a new age may lead to the establishment of a defacto New World Order, but not under the leadership of the Lord Jesus Christ. Ultimately, therefore, it will lead into eternal damnation.

The movement is not a single organization, but is a vast network of groups that are promoting "mind sciences" and the concept of the **"Age of Aquarius"** or the New World Order. The groupings may be religious, political, philosophical, educational, or scientific.

For example, new "churches" have sprung up, calling themselves "The Church of the Sacred Heart of Maitreya." It is the creation of "Shan the Rising Light," which claims to be a "religious, spiritual, philosophical focus, manifesting

the Rising Light of Maitreya Buddha and the Divine Will of
Michael the Archangel through the grail of Man!"

What are the essential components?

1. It is a religion, because it seeks to discover the origin
of truth.

2. It seeks to inquire about people's inner conscious-
ness and past lives through past regression and hypnosis
analysis.

3. Techniques of meditation, holistic healing, and acu-
puncture are used.

4. The movement claims to have reached those who are
deceased.

5. The use of LSD and marijuana to put one's self
temporarily with the higher self.

6. The movement claims that Buddha, Lao Tse, Jesus,
and other enlightened teachers were all the same reincar-
nated person.

7. Christian principles must be discredited and abandoned. Christianity and all other religions are to become an
integral part of the New Age World Religion. Christians
who resist the plan will be dealt with. If necessary, they will
be exterminated and the world "purified."

8. Children are to be spiritually seduced and indoctri-
nated, and the classroom used to promote new age dogma.[18]

As in all homemade, self-invented religions, material
objects play an important role in the New Age religion. Like
other sects, many New Age groups attach importance to
artifacts, relics, and sacred objects like Tibetan bells, solar
energizers, and colored stones and crystals.

Crystals are not only thought to have mysterious healing powers, but are also considered to be programmable like
a computer. They say different levels of your body relate to
different stones — e.g., amethyst quartz controls the temperature, enhances mental clarity and strengthens will-
power. It is excellent for meditation. Rose quartz is the
healing stone, clear quartz alleviates emotional extremes,

while smoky quartz is the powerful crystal used for purifying the energy center of the body.[19]

The New Age movement is potentially the greatest threat to the young people of the nation. Instead of looking to God's Word for the answers to life, and placing their faith and trust in Him, tens of thousands of people everywhere are taking hold of any type of religion that seems to promise a better future, a better self, and eternal security — a sort of "do your own thing and control your own destiny."

Clearly, the plan is to create a world order in which not only churches and religions, but all of society will be controlled by the Lord Maitreya — or the Antichrist. (The word Maitreya means master.)

Within this massive worldwide network of the New Age movement, there is a clear satanic conspiracy which is working to bring about a counterfeit kingdom of Christ. The term "Christ" is being used widely, referring to a spiritual master who will usher in, and lead the world into, the tranquil Age of Aquarius.

One of the leading lights of the movement is a man named David Spangler. He is a member of the board of directors of Planetary Citizens — a prestigious organization with headquarters at the U.N. in New York. In his book, *Reflections on the Christ*, Spangler makes it clear that the coming new age requires a Luciferic initiation. He says:

> The true light of Lucifer cannot be seen through sorrow, through darkness, through rejection. The true light of this great being can only be recognized when one's eyes can see with the light of the Christ, the light of the inner sun. Lucifer works within each of us to bring us to wholeness, and as we move into a new age, which is the age of man's wholeness, each of us in some way is brought to that point which I term the Luciferic initiation, the particular doorway through which the individual must pass if

> he is to come fully into the presence of his light and his wholeness.
>
> Lucifer comes to give us the final gift of wholeness. If we accept it, then he is free and we are free. That is the Luciferic initiation. It is one that many people now, and in the days ahead will be facing, for it is an initiation into the **New Age.**[20]

Luciferians such as Spangler, of course, claim that Lucifer is the Christ; in spite of the general understanding and the dictionary definition of Lucifer being Satan (shining one).

Believers (born-again Christians) know the **TRUTH** because they have God's Word which is truth, and it is that truth that warns us of a great deception with the coming of the man of lawlessness (Antichrist).

We read in 2 Thessalonians 2:9-10:

> The coming of the lawless one will be in accordance with the work of Satan displayed in all kinds of counterfeit miracles, signs and wonders, and in every sort of evil that deceives those who are perishing. They perish because they refused to love the truth and so be saved.

The implications for the Christian are horrific. But the Word of God is our comfort. Matthew 24:13 says: "He who stands firm to the end will be saved."

The Bible also warns the believer about the "false prophets" in the end times. Matthew 24:24 says: "For false Christs and false prophets will appear and perform great signs and miracles to deceive even the elect — if that were possible."

This New Age movement is radically opposed to the traditional and evangelical interpretation of the Bible. Their interpretation of the next great event in the prophetic calendar — the Rapture is: "At last we will be rid of these

Christians who have been transported to another planet for re-education."

I believe we are seeing today the rapid growth in "way-out" heathen beliefs in the name of religion, because the time of Christ's coming is at hand.

66. Question: Will there ever be a "one world religion"?

Answer: There are ominous signs on the skyline today which warn us of the dangerous direction in which events are moving in some ecumenical circles. On the occasion of the Pope's visit to Australia in September 1989, the headline in one local newspaper read: "Pope 'Welcomed' as Head of Unified Church." The report went on to say: "Most Brisbane Anglicans would welcome reunion with the Roman Catholic church, a city Anglican priest said yesterday. The Rev. Fr. Walter Ogle said most Anglicans (formally known as the Church of England) would be willing to accept the Pope's authority as head of a reunited church."[21]

Again, similar thoughts were expressed when the Pope visited Australia in January 1995.

In January 1989, the former prime minister of Australia, Mr. Robert Hawke, gave the welcoming speech to 600 delegates attending the fifth assembly of the World Conference on Religion and Peace at Monash University, Melbourne, Australia. Mr. Hawke, an avowed atheist, said that he did not feel uncomfortable addressing the assembly representing the major religions of the world, including Jews, Buddhists, Hindus, Moslems, Mormons, and the Christian denominations.[22]

There is further evidence to suggest that a one-world religion is very likely within the next decade when we see a growing ecumenical tendency between the Roman Catholic church and the Muslim faith.

In order for anti-Christianity to become the exclusive world religion, all other existing religions must be taken into consideration. This is very much in accordance with Scripture, and this ecumenical spirit will lead to the fulfillment of Revelation 17:13: "They have one purpose (or they are of one mind) and will give their power and authority to the beast." This satanic imitation of the perfect unity of the body of Christ can be observed in various religions today. All claim to believe in the one true God, thus opening the door for communication, dialogue, and finally compromise.

Now, on the surface, this tendency is justified by the Bible. Look at 1 Timothy 2:5: "For there is one God," but the next sentence identifies the fatal error of the visible unity-seeking movement: "And one mediator between God and men, the man Christ Jesus."

Only Christianity Recognizes the Deity of Jesus Christ

Many of the religious bodies throughout the world are more or less already united in their acceptance of the state-church — such as **the Vatican.** All major denominations are in dialogue with the Vatican, with the aim of uniting Christendom under one denominator.[23] The Pope, who is the spiritual leader of this vast empire, is at the same time a political leader of the nation called "The Vatican." He, as head, is eager to unite other religions such as — Muslims, Hinduism, Buddhism, Bahal, etc., into a cooperative union that would respect each other's beliefs.

But the Bible message is plain and clear:

> Neither is there salvation in any other: for there is none other name under heaven given among men, whereby we must be saved (Acts 4:12;KJV).

In recent times, we have seen emerging through legislatures a school of thought which says that by teaching Scripture we are discriminating against other religions. This disturbing trend may well give rise to "vilification laws" which prevent the preaching of the gospel, certainly in public places, unless it is done under the auspices of a world church. Pointers to this are to be seen in China and some other countries today. For this very reason the Lord warned us, "Work . . . while it is day: the night cometh, when no man can work" (John 9:4;KJV).

We know a time is coming when the people will accept a one-world religion. It will be consummated during the Tribulation period. However, what is vitally needed today, before Christ takes the Church to glory, are millions of believers who will remain steadfast and true to their convictions, no matter what pressures or persecutions may come.

Surely we can do no better than to adopt as our aim in this life the challenging words penned by Martin Luther more than 450 years ago:

> If I profess with the loudest voice and the clearest exposition every portion of the truth of God, except precisely that little point which the world and the devil are at that moment attacking, I am not confessing Christ, however boldly I may be professing Christ. Where the battle rages, there the loyalty of the soldier is proved, and to be steady on all the battle fields besides is mere flight and disgrace if he flinches at that point.

67. Question: What is this dominion theology being taught in seminar groups and in our schools today?

Answer: When Jesus returns for the second time, He will extend the heavenly order to earth so that the will of God will be done on earth as it is in heaven. Today, however, we are witnessing the emergence of a misguided and heretical doctrine which I believe is one of the most dangerous trends in Evangelical Christianity.

Dominion theology, has two arms or strands to its ideology:

1. Christian reconstruction
2. Kingdom Now

Essentially, what the doctrine is saying is that Christians have been given the authority from the Word of God to turn the world around, by force if necessary. They have been given a mandate to politically reconstruct the world and to take *dominion* over the planet, thus establishing the **kingdom of God NOW** on earth, before Christ returns.

When we analyze their doctrine in the light of the literal interpretation of Scripture, we see that dominionists are wrong on both of their major thrusts:

1. They are wrong about the timing of the Kingdom — i.e., their "Kingdom Now" philosophy.

2. They are wrong about the means of establishing the Kingdom: they believe that the Kingdom is established by the work of the Church rather than through Christ and His return.

What does the Word of God say? The Scriptures could not be clearer. It says that Christians are to seek after the things above and not after earthly things (Col. 3:1-2), while we eagerly await our Saviour's return (Phil. 3:20).

At creation, man was given dominion over all other living things (Gen. 1:26,28). Note: Mankind was not included. No one man or group was ever given the sole right to rule the world. Our calling in the present is not to take dominion over the world, but rather to preach the gospel to the world (Matt. 28:19), and to occupy until Jesus comes to deliver us from the wrath to come (1 Thess. 1:10).

How does the reconstructionists' view of end-time prophecy differ from that of the fundamental literal Christian view?

1. The Rapture: There is no distinction between the two events — the Rapture and the Second Coming.

2. The Second Coming: It will take place at the end of the Millennium or Kingdom.

3. The Last Days: The term applies to Israel only and occurred between Christ's first coming and the A.D. 70 destruction of Jerusalem.

4. The Tribulation Judgments: They took place when Israel fell in A.D. 70. Naturally, they say there is no future for the nation of Israel.

5. The Great Apostasy: This happened in the first century. Therefore we should expect increasing Christianization of the world, not increasing apostasy.

6. The Beast of Revelation: This was a symbol of Nero and the Roman Empire.

7. The False Prophet of Revelation: He was the leader of an apostate Israel.

8. The Antichrist: It is a term to describe the widespread apostasy of the Church prior to the fall of Jerusalem. They do not consider the word refers to a future person.

9. The Millennium: This is the present reign of Christians as kings on earth in the Kingdom established by Christ at His first coming.

10. The Thousand Years of Revelation 20: This is a large rounded-off number containing the idea of a fullness of quantity. It may represent a million years — amazing!

11. The New Heavens and New Earth: This has already begun as our salvation in Christ, both now and in eternity. The new Jerusalem is the Church now and forever!

12. Armageddon: This will never be a literal battle since the Christian reconstruction movement says there is no such place. It signifies the defeat of those who set themselves against God.[24]

68. Question: Will the world be destroyed by the "greenhouse effect"? What relation does this have to the depletion of the ozone layer?

Answer: People across the globe are worried about the greenhouse effect and the "hole" in the ozone layer. Some scientists are not fazed by recent public interest, while others are concerned to such a degree that they are prepared to state that the world will one day be destroyed by a combination of dangerous pollutants in the atmosphere.

Nature produces many gases which together form the air we breathe. These include oxygen, carbon dioxide, nitrogen, water vapor, methane, and ozone.

Some gases, especially carbon dioxide, also keep the sun's warmth in a kind of greenhouse around the world. Without it the world would be too cold to live in. On earth, trees and other plants "breathe in" carbon dioxide and "breathe out" oxygen, the gas all living creatures need most of all. This still leaves enough carbon dioxide in the atmosphere to keep the world at the right temperature.

The Big Burn Off

Until the twentieth century the natural process worked very well. With advancements in technology, man began to burn huge quantities of coal, petroleum products, and timber. These raw materials were required for transport, heating, lighting, cooking, and many other purposes.

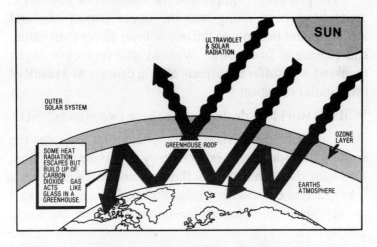

ULTRAVIOLET & SOLAR RADIATION

SUN

OUTER SOLAR SYSTEM

GREENHOUSE ROOF

OZONE LAYER

SOME HEAT RADIATION ESCAPES BUT BUILD UP OF CARBON DIOXIDE GAS ACTS LIKE GLASS IN A GREENHOUSE.

EARTHS ATMOSPHERE

Diagram 3. Greenhouse Effect

However, waste gases from this big burn-off contain far more carbon dioxide than nature can absorb through the remaining trees on earth. So more and more of that gas is accumulating in the atmosphere and increasing the greenhouse effect.

As a result, spaceship earth's temperature is rising, not just above the places where the gases are produced, but all over the world. This rising temperature is expected to produce erratic weather patterns, higher sea levels, more frequent storms, and various other effects on nature and the environment.

The Ozone Holes

Above the greenhouse layer, there is another layer of atmospheric gas called ozone, which nature also releases from the earth. This gas has the property or ability to absorb the dangerous ultra-violet rays which come from the sun.

This ozone layer surrounding the earth is very thin, and is easily damaged by other gases containing compounds of chlorine, such as chloro-fluoro-carbon — CFC. This gas is man-made, and is used in aerosols, refrigerators, and other products.

The problem is simply that for a number of years CFC gases have been rising into the upper atmosphere and attacking and destroying the ozone layer faster than nature can replace it from earth. Without this protective layer, mankind will suffer the effects of skin cancers as a result of ultra-violet radiation.[25]

Will the world be destroyed by these two effects? NO!

I don't read anywhere in prophecy that indicates the world will be destroyed other than by the divine act of God. This won't happen until after the Millennium. BUT — what I do see is a cause-effect relationship. Because of man's greed without due concern for the environment, the world will suffer many problems as the time draws towards the end of this age — "the Church Age."

The greenhouse effect and the depletion of the ozone layer are the current popular fears. But what the world fears today is nothing compared to what it will experience during the great Tribulation judgments (Rev. 6-19).

What does the Word of God have to say?

It is not without reason that the Lord specifically mentioned "the sea and the waves roaring."

> "There will be signs in the sun, moon, and stars. On the earth, nations will be in anguish and perplexity at the roaring and tossing of the sea" (Luke 21:25).

One of the great fears of the greenhouse effect is the potential for sea-levels to rise, and for oceans tides to become stronger due to the increased heat from temperature rises around the world. If this should happen low-lying coastal lands and islands would be flooded and disappear. This is another prediction of the end-time judgments as recorded in the book of Revelation 16:20.

Summarizing: It is obvious that such a statement relating to nature was meant to call our attention to the waters of the world that we may know and understand that even they bring the message that the Lord is coming.

When the Son of God hung on Calvary's cross, we read that "there was darkness over the whole land" (Mark 15:33), and "the earth shook and the rocks split" (Matt. 27:51). At this scene, nature gave forth signs to such an extent that even the hardened Roman soldiers, as well as the opposing religious people, had to recognize that this righteous man controlled the elements and nature (Luke 23:47-48).

A definite parallel can be drawn between this scene at Calvary and the Tribulation judgments. During these judgments, men's hearts will be so evil that they will again curse God as they did at the Cross (Rev. 16:9,21).

69. Question: How serious is the rising tide of Muslim extremism which threatens to engulf much of the developing world?

Answer: The seeds of the present revival can be traced back as far as the 1800s and to the period of western colonialism. However, it was in the 1970s and 1980s that the revival has gained its greatest impetus. As the countries of the world come closer together in terms of communications, Muslims have become exposed to the social structures and lifestyles which they view as totally alien. Their frustration is heightened by the fact that most of the Muslim countries must deal with European and western civilization for economic survival. This to a large degree has created a fear among the more fundamental religious groups who now see adherence to the strict Islamic culture as a means of ultimate supremacy in the world.

When the pro-western Shah of Iran (Persia) was deposed in 1979, power fell into the hands of the ayatollahs. The ayatollah Khomeini, who returned from exile in France had, until his death in 1989, exerted power and influence over Muslim people far beyond the boundaries of his own country. His statement, "Islam was dead or dying for nearly 14 centuries, but we have revived it with the blood of our youth. . . . We shall soon liberate Jerusalem and pray there," has helped to inflame the Islamic revolution for domination of the world.[26]

The controversial publication by Simon Rushdie, "Satanic Verses," has in a significant way both angered and united the Muslims. Essentially what has happened is that Rushdie has exposed the fallacies of Islam. Other commentators have raised various questions concerning the validity of the Muslims sacred scriptures — the Koran, and many of the claims surrounding the prophet Mohammed — the founder of the faith.

Islam beliefs rest on their statement of faith: "There

is no 'other' God but Allah, and Mohammed is his prophet."

Their teachings accept there were other prophets before Mohammed and that Jesus was one of them. However, the Koran emphatically denies that Jesus was God in human flesh.

What does the Word of God say?

> Many deceivers, who do not acknowledge Jesus Christ as coming in the flesh, have gone out into the world. Any such person is the deceiver and the antichrist (2 John 7).

> Who is the liar? It is the man who denies that Jesus is the Christ. Such a man is the antichrist — he denies the Father and the Son (1 John 2:22).

The Scripture confirms the falsehood of Islam. It is blatantly antichrist in essence and theology, and this latest resurgence and escalation in worldwide Islamic activity is just another clear indication that we are living in the last days.

Yes! The activity of Islam is serious but is just part of the worldwide disturbances and violence predicted in the Bible. It will, however, be found wanting at Christ's return. The sad part is that millions will go to a lost eternity because of their denial of Jesus Christ.

70. Question: Can we understand Islamic fundamentalism?

Answer: The influence of Islam in the Middle East conflict is foundational. To ignore the demands of Islam in the region is to waste ones time at any peace efforts.

Islam considers God originally gave the land of Israel to the Jews but because of disobedience that title deed has been transferred to the now rightful owners — the Muslim people. The Koran clearly states that the land of Israel is Islam's possession until "Judgment Day." Therefore, any

Arab group that makes peace with Israel on the grounds of mutual recognition and co-existence negates every Islamic — and by definition, Arab — principle.

They are considered a traitor to the will of god (Allah) and deserving of death.

Islam will never be persuaded to depart from this position. Indeed, for her to do so would be to surrender the credibility of her entire revelation. Therefore, in essence, the conflict in the Middle East is about the true revelation of God and His promised blessings. It is a conflict between the Torah and the Koran. For this reason Islam has to work towards the total destruction of Israel. Only such a destruction will verify her revelation.

This reality puts the present rise of Islamic fundamentalism into proper perspective and it makes Islam the real danger to world peace. She will not and cannot stop until Israel is destroyed and her recent drive to acquire nuclear capability is proof of it.

What Does Islam Teach?

They have "five pillars" of faith and practice:

1. Confessing that there is no god but Allah, and Muhammad is his prophet.

2. Performing prayer five times a day facing Mecca under strict procedural guidelines and posture, along with a precisely repeated set of words.

3. Giving of alms to the needy.

4. Keeping a fast during daylight hours for one particular month of the year — the Feast of Ramadan.

5. If possible, once in a lifetime, making a pilgrimage (*hajji*) to Mecca.

When we compare the Koran with the Bible, we observe that Islam recognizes Jesus as another prophet, inferior to Muhammad, born of a virgin, performed miracles, and lived a sinless life, according to their Koran. But they do not believe in Christ's deity, atoning death, and resurrection. They teach a works-salvation religion, even militant and at times a cruel view of heaven, which is also carnal, sensuous, and lustful. They assume that the Old Testament has been corrupted by the Jews and the New Testament by Christians. Their Koran, they believe is accurate in every detail, even with its questionable origin and history.

Since its beginning in the seventh century A.D. in Arabia, followers of Islam have been at odds with Christians, Jews, and Hindus. It has become known as a "religion of the sword." There is little love in its charter. The Koran does not teach an unconditional love of God but rather that God only loves those who love Him.

It is important to understand that Islam is a legal system rather than a religion based on articles of faith. The Muslim is not saved because he believes in something. He merely observes Islamic practices and regards Islam as his identity and loyalty.

The final aim of fundamental Islam is to see the whole of the world as dar-al-Islam, the "Home of Islam." The bottom line in Islam's philosophy is simple. There can be no secular democratic Palestinian Arab state in which Muslims, Christians, and Jews share the same rights. Moreover, Muhammad himself wrote that "Islam is always superior, nothing can be superior over it."

With this stated aim, the conclusion that there never can or will be lasting peace in the Middle East is to state the obvious.

71. Question: We hear almost daily in the news about radical elements called Hamas and Hezbollah. Who are they?

Answer: During the late 1980s and by the early 1990s, communism as a force exporting terror and social unrest had been neutralized. At the same time, terrorism was spreading like a cancer from its base in Tehran, Iran. Unlike the political force directed from Moscow, the beast now to be reckoned with was a spiritual movement. Fundamentalist Islam has become the exporter of violence and social unrest among the nations in the Middle East.

The *modus-operandi* of Islamic conquest is to stir, within the masses, dissension towards a nation's current government policies, and to present the ideals of religious fundamentalism as the best alternative system to achieve a nation's political and social aspirations. A case in point is the Palestinian (P.L.O.) uprising in Israel which began in 1987 and is referred to as the *intifada.*

Within the PLO and their associated terrorist organizations, dissident factions who would be considered extreme militant groups have surfaced. They believe that armed struggle is the only way to liberate Palestine. Operating from different points within and outside Israel, these groups all have a common agenda:

1. They are all fully committed to the total destruction of Israel.
2. They are all backed and armed by the Syrian-Iran Alliance.
3. They are all motivated by Islamic Fundamentalism.

There are two main organizations among a number of dissident P.L.O. factions and popular "front" groups.

Hamas — an Arabic acronym for the "Islamic Resistance Movement." Hamas is a *Sunni* Muslim Palestinian terrorist organization openly dedicated to destroying any peace opportunities between Israel, the secular Arab countries on her borders, and the Palestinians.

Article 9 of the Palestinian National Covenant states clearly their aim: "Armed struggle is the only way to liberate Palestine and is therefore a strategy and not a tactic."

Hezbollah — which means "Party of God" is a radical

shi'ite terrorist organization operating from Lebanon and dedicated to the creation of an Iranian-style Islamic republic in Lebanon and the removal of all non-Islamic influences from the area. Their aim is also one of de-stabilization through periodic shelling of Israeli towns in the northern Galilee region, as well as *"kamikaze"* style raids into Israeli territory.

Both organizations are fanatic and militant extremist arms of Islamic fundamentalism backed financially and spiritually by Iran.

These terror groups will never accept anything short of Israel's destruction, and their commitment, if any, to a peace agreement is only a mechanism to buy time so as to pursue more vehemently their assault against Israel.

It is interesting to note that the Bible had already foreshadowed such a situation would arise. Psalm 83:3-5 says:

> With cunning they conspire against your people; they plot against those you cherish. "Come," they say, "let us destroy them as a nation, that the name of Israel be remembered no more." With one mind they plot together; they form an alliance against you.

Even considering the current climate and expectations of peace among the leaders of Israel, Jordan, and the P.L.O., I believe we shall also observe at some future time, a massive army involving Islamic/Arab forces gathering to surround Jerusalem. It is when this happens, the Bible tells us, that the Lord will intervene on behalf of His chosen people, the Jews, and the words of the prophet as recorded in Zechariah 12:3 will finally be fulfilled:

> On that day, when all the nations of the earth are gathered against her, I will make Jerusalem an immovable rock for all the nations. All

who try to move it will injure themselves.

ISRAEL: God's Chief Obstacle to Islamic Supremacy in the Middle East

It is somewhat of a paradox, but the major obstacle to an Islamic overthrow of secular Arab governments throughout the Middle East is the tiny nation of Israel.

Without Israel's protective umbrella and military superiority, thanks largely to the United States of America and other allies, neighboring countries like Lebanon and Jordan might well be easy prey for invading fanatical Islamic hordes organized and directed from Iran. Therefore the neutralization of Israel as an effective force to be reckoned with becomes essential in any plan to ensure the final victory of Islam against secular nationalism in the Arab states.

For this reason, the Palestine Liberation Organization (P.L.O.) claims Iran has "hijacked" the *intifada* or Palestinian uprising in Israel. Relations between Yassir Arafat's P.L.O. and the fanatical Islamic fundamentalists from Iran could only be described as lukewarm. Hamas and Hezbullah terrorist attacks are aimed at stopping the peace process and starting a war between Israel and her Arab neighbors.

An Islamic army needs no incentive to attack Israel other than the Koran's command to wage *jihad*, or holy war in the name of Islam. Israel unfortunately has to bear the brunt of Islamic aggression for one simple but obvious reason. She is perceived by the leaders of Islam to be an extension of the West. Israel is the whipping post in the Middle East for Islam's grievances against the West. We saw vivid evidence of this during the Gulf War when Saddam Hussein, the military dictator from Iraq cried *jihad* and then launched Scud missile attacks against the infidel Israel in response to the Allied attack.

The Arab Verses Persian Conflict

A further obstacle confronting the Muslim world in the

Middle East is the internal division over the long-standing ethnic dispute between the Persians and Arabs. Again we saw evidence of this with the eight-year war between Iran and Iraq during the 1980s.

Historically, the primary insult to an Arab living in the Middle East is to call him a Persian. Conversely, a slap in the face to a Persian is being referred to as an Arab. However, this apparent barrier is gradually breaking down. The day is fast approaching when fundamentalist Arabs and Persians may lay their ethnic differences aside and re-dedicate themselves to the common Islamic cause and goal — the destruction of the Jewish state.

Hamas, operating from within the borders of Israel, and **Hezbollah**, from without, show all the characteristics and signs of being the forerunners of such a beastly alliance. Maybe this is precisely the strategy Iran is formulating to strike at the West. First, neutralize Arab nationalistic goals and then go for the jugular by installing Islamic rule in Jerusalem. Despite their long standing differences, both the Arab Sunnis and the mainly Persian Shi'ites share a common vision, and that is Muslim rule in Jerusalem. Whatever may be the final outcome, I believe we won't have long to wait.

72. Question: Who are the Palestinians?

Answer: The name Palestine is a corruption of the word "Philistine," a seafaring people who more than likely originated from the island of Crete in the Mediterranean. They invaded the coast of the land of Canaan around 1200 B.C., shortly after the Jewish conquest under the leadership of Joshua. The main Philistine dominions never extended much further than the coastal strip between Gaza and the modern city of Tel Aviv. The Philistines disappeared as a people under the heel of the Babylonians around 600 B.C. It was the Roman Empire Hadrian, bent on destroying every vestige of Jewish attachment to the land, that invented the name "Palestina" to replace Judea, the historic name of the country.

While this Roman name disappeared in the land itself shortly after the conquest by the Moslems, Christian cartographers kept the name alive in their own lands and eventually bequeathed it to the allied negotiators at Versailles and the inhabitants of the land. The name was never used officially, and had no precise territorial definition until it was adopted by the British to designate the area which they acquired by conquest at the end of World War I.

Just prior to the rebirth of the nation of Israel in May 1948, the Arab propaganda machine instructed the Arab people living in Palestine to flee to Gaza and/or Jordan. This they did on the basis that within a short time after nationhood, Israel would suffer defeat and be eliminated. Following this assumed brief skirmish resulting in Arab victory, all the people who temporarily left would then be able to return and claim the land forever. This never happened.

A displaced Arab population of about 600,000 were then allowed to languish in refugee camps from 1948 to 1967. This happened in spite of their Arab brothers, who with incredible oil wealth never held out the hand of friendship. Their own brethren disowned them since they perceived their usefulness in the ongoing campaign against Israel. They became the cannon fodder of the Arab cause.

Thus, in 1964 a decision was taken by the P.L.O. to create a new identity for them. They would no longer be married to the Arab family but would henceforth claim a separate identity as Palestinians.

In 1967, Israel, in a war of survival, acquired the West Bank, Gaza, and Old Jerusalem, and with these regions they inherited the Palestinian people as well. Constant attempts by the Israelis to improve their conditions were rejected by the Palestinian leadership, the Arab world, and the United Nations.

Naturally, a new generation of Palestinians has grown

up with an intense hate for Israel. Considering their traumatic history one can only have compassion for them. In all, they are the hopeless victims of hate-filled masters, the P.L.O.

73. Question: Who are the remnant of Edom?

Answer: When we study the Old Testament in detail, we notice that more judgment has been levied against the country of Edom than any other nation other than Babylon.

The prophet Amos had this to say in chapter 9:11-12:

> "In that day I will restore David's fallen tent.
> I will repair its broken places, restore its ruins, and
> build it as it used to be, so that they may possess the
> remnant of Edom and all the nations that bear my
> name," declares the Lord, who will do these things.

Who are the Edomites?

They are the descendants of Esau, the first-born son of Isaac whose father was Abraham (Gen. 36:40). Among the many wives that Esau took from among the women of Canaan was Basemath the daughter of Ishmael, Abraham's son born of an Egyptian woman named Hagar, who became the father of the Arab people (Gen. 36:3).

The problem in the Middle East today is a struggle between the descendants of Jacob and the descendants of Esau and Ishmael.

Esau, who became the father of the Edomites moved out from the land of Canaan and settled in the hill country of Seir near Wadi Musa or Petra which became known as the territory of Edom in modern day Jordan (Gen. 36:7).

When Judah was weak as a result of the Babylonian captivity around 590 B.C., the Edomites moved out of Bozrah in Petra en masse back into Judah, the southern area of the land of Israel (Isa. 63:1).

History shows that this relocation by the Edomites was due in part to an attack by a group of tribal Arabians called

Nabataeans (descendants of Ishmael) who moved into Petra about the same time the Babylonians were invading Israel (Ps. 137:7).

The most famous Edomite mentioned in the Bible was Herod the Great. Being half-Jew and half-Edomite, one can understand why he was hated by the Jews at the time of Christ.

When the Roman general Titus finally sacked Jerusalem and dispersed the Jews in A.D. 70, many of the Edomites were also dispersed. Large numbers moved out of Palestine and settled in the Balkans — modern day Yugoslavia, Albania, and Bulgaria. This area has been known for many years as the "Powder Keg of Europe." Those who remained in Palestine formed the remnant of Esau (Edom), who today are referred to as the Palestinian Arabs.

Where is the remnant of Edom today?

1. Palestinian Arabs in Gaza and Jordan — who have no legitimate claim to Israel.

2. In the Balkans. The people of Bozrah in Edom were known as Bosnians. Where are the Bosnians today? They are an ethnic group in Yugoslavia, a country under the judgment of war.

I believe the Palestinians surrounding the nation of Israel are about to receive their judgment if they continue with the *intifada*.

Hitler and Yassir Arafat

In 1917, General Allenby defeated the Turkish armies in the Jezreel Valley. That proved to be the downfall of the Turks in the Middle East. He then continued on towards Jerusalem and captured the city without a fight. As he rode towards the Jaffa Gate, Allenby dismounted from his white horse. One of his aides asked, "General Allenby, are you not going to ride into Jerusalem and take the surrender?"

"No," replied Allenby, "My Saviour Jesus Christ will do that." You see, Allenby was a born-again Christian. He walked in through the Jaffa Gate and took the surrender without a fight in the Western Wall Square.

Standing in the square was a man by the name of Husseni-El-Husseni. Allenby said to this man, "Husseni-El-Husseni, you are now the mayor of Jerusalem." Standing beside Husseni was a young boy by the name of Aman-El-Husseni. In the process of time, Aman-El-Husseni grew up to be an influential leader among his Arab people in Palestine. He took a pilgrimage to Mecca and became the *hajji* Aman-El-Husseni.

In the early 1940s Adolf Hitler invited *hajji* Aman-El-Husseni to come to Germany to discuss the "final solution" for the Jewish people in Palestine. Hitler invited Husseni to go over to Bosnia and pick up some friends and take them back to Palestine to help in that final solution.

Hajji Aman-El-Husseni is the uncle of Yassir Arafat — the head of the P.L.O., a terrorist organization following after blood. Not wanting to serve the younger brother. Still wanting back the birthright — a piece of property called *eretz* Israel — the land of Israel.

But the Bible says it's God's land and it is reserved for the people of God, the Jews. Leviticus 25:23 says: " 'The land must not be sold permanently, because the land is mine and you are but aliens and my tenants.' "

The prophet Ezekiel in chapter 37:12-14 made it very clear on this issue of land, the central conflict in the Middle East today:

> "Therefore prophesy and say to them: 'This is what the Sovereign Lord says: O my people, I am going to open your graves and bring you up from them; I will bring you back to the land of Israel. Then you, my people, will know that I am the Lord, when I open your graves and bring you up from them. I will put my Spirit in you and you will live, and I will settle you in your own land. Then you will know that I the Lord have spoken, and I

have done it, declares the Lord.' "

74. Question: Can we expect a nuclear war in which countries around the Middle East will be destroyed?

Answer: The simple answer to this question is **YES!** There will be limited use of nuclear weapons used during the future world wars; and **NO!** The world will not be destroyed by man and his war games. God will destroy this world only after the millennial reign of His Son Jesus Christ (refer to chart 10, page 137.)

As we carefully observe the current events around the globe, I believe we are standing on the threshold of an imploding society. Man's quest for power and supremacy, driven by an unquenchable desire and greed, will finally be his "Waterloo."

It is not without coincidence that the father of the nuclear (atom) bomb was a Jew — Albert Einstein. But because the Jews rejected the Messiah, they are to be judged, and part of those future judgments will involve nuclear weapons in some form or another.

How do we know the Jews and their enemies will suffer a nuclear attack?

Simply — the Scriptures tell us. In the Book of Zechariah we read the following:

> This is the plague with which the Lord will strike all the nations that fought against Jerusalem: Their flesh will rot while they are still standing on their feet, their eyes will rot in their sockets, and their tongues will rot in their mouths (Zech. 14:12).

This is an exact description of the effects of radiation poisoning.

What nation does this prophecy refer to?

This prophecy is directed against all the nations attacking the Jews in their land. It will apparently happen on Jewish soil, at God's direction, and at the time just prior to the return of Jesus Christ to planet Earth. It is quite possible that "the battle or campaign of Armageddon" will see the use of a limited nuclear attack. I say "limited" because in the same chapter we are told there are survivors who will inhabit the earthly millennial kingdom (Zech. 14:16).

If there was to be a full scale nuclear war, very little human life and uncontaminated materials would remain at a time when Jesus Christ would be setting up His earthly reign. It is most likely from the biblical reference in 2 Peter 3:10, that the earth will be finally destroyed by God using nuclear means, but we need to remember that this total destruction of this earth will only take place after the millennial reign of Jesus Christ.

75. Question: Does the Golan Heights belong to Israel or Syria?

Answer: There are many current emotive issues that occupy the minds and hearts of Jewish people. None more so than the question of the Golan.

When Israel obtained nationhood in 1948, the Golan Heights was already settled and administered by Syria. As a result of the 1967 war, Israel gained back the territories of East Jerusalem and the Golan it once occupied in the days before the diaspora in A.D. 70.

Gaza was also claimed, but historically never formed part of Israel. It was the territory of the Philistines — God's instrument of judgment for His disobedient people.

The territory on the Golan once occupied by Syria was just a wasteland and virtually of no significant value to them. The population consisted of a few Druse villages and the Syrian government's only interest in the area was for the harassment of Israeli farmers in the Kibitzes along the shore of Lake Galilee and in the rich farmlands of the Hula Valley.

Since the Six-Day War in 1967, there has been a

remarkable change to the landscape on the Golan. The country is stocked with cattle. Large settlements and ultra-modern towns dot the countryside. Small crop farming is in abundance. Surely the prophet Ezekiel was speaking of such a time when he exclaimed: "They will say, 'This land that was laid waste has become like the garden of Eden; the cities that were lying in ruins, desolate and destroyed, are now fortified and inhabited' " (Ezek. 36:35).

The Golan always belonged to Israel

In Joshua 21:27 we read "The Levite clans of the Gershonites were given: from the half-tribe of Manasseh, Golan in Bashan (a city of refuge for one accused of murder) and Be Eshtarah, together with their pasture-lands — two towns."

It is interesting to note that God in His grace determined that one of the cities of refuge was to be on the Golan. The fact that Israel would even contemplate giving away this part of the Promised Land shows how far the level of deception has reached the minds and hearts of the politicians in the Knesset — the Israeli Parliament. **The Golan was never a part of Syria**. It only came into existence as such as a result of planning by Britain and France after World War I. Syria has no claim, politically, historically, or morally to this part of Israel's territory.

The Golan Heights is also referred to in the Bible as Bashan and is part of the ancient inheritance of the House of Israel. Deuteronomy 4:43 says: "The cities were these: Bezer in the desert plateau, for the Reubenites; Ramoth in Gilead, for the Gadites; and Golan in Bashan, for the Manassites."

The Manassites were one of the 12 tribes of Israel. First Chronicles 6:71 says: "The Gershonites received the following: From the clan of the half-tribe of Manasseh they received Golan in Bashan and also Ashtaroth, together with their pasture-lands."

The Golan is also part of the prophetic fulfillment of

Israel's return to the land, and a place of promised blessings and restoration:

> But I will bring Israel back to his own pasture and he will graze on Carmel and Bashan; his appetite will be satisfied on the hills of Ephraim and Gilead (Jer. 50:19).

> Shepherd your people with your staff, the flock of your inheritance, which lives by itself in a forest, in fertile pasture-lands. Let them feed in Bashan and Gilead as in days long ago (Mic. 7:14).

76. Question: Is there any truth in the belief that the Jewish temple must be built before Christ returns?

Answer: This is a somewhat popular question but can at the same time be a confusing one. We must first differentiate between the two stages of Christ's coming. Firstly, He comes **for** His saints, the event known as the Rapture; and secondly, Christ finally returns **with** His saints.

The interval of time between the two stages of His second coming will be seven years, during which time the great Tribulation judgments occur on earth.

To answer the question directly — **NO!** There is nothing which prevents Jesus Christ coming for His bride — the Church. The temple certainly does not have to be built prior to this event taking place.

There is only an indirect relationship between the Church and the physical temple. The Church is God's mystery to the Jews and His Son's bride. The Church consists of people. It is not a building. The building often referred to as the Church is only a rain shelter. But the Bible tells us that the temple of the Holy Spirit — the third person of the Trinity is the body of believers.

The apostle Paul reveals in 1 Corinthians 6:19: "Do you

not know that your body is a temple of the Holy Spirit, who is in you, whom you have received from God? You are not your own."

On the other hand, the building called the temple is a physical structure for people to worship in. It is uniquely Jewish and will play a major part in the end-time events on this earth during the Tribulation period.

To answer the second part of the question — **YES!** The temple must be rebuilt before Christ returns physically to this earth to reign as King of kings. (Refer to question 17, page 44.)

The Red Heifer

An interesting aspect relating to the third temple — the temple of the Tribulation period is as follows: According to Numbers 19 and a cross reference in Hebrews 9, the Lord instructed Moses and Aaron that the red heifer was to be slain outside the camp by Eliezer the priest, and its ashes were to be used for cleansing and purification.[27]

Serious Jewish religious leaders in Jerusalem believe that the construction of the third temple cannot begin before these ashes are found, as those involved must be ceremonially cleansed before true temple worship can take place. According to the Scriptures, the ashes, mixed with water, purify. So Jewish scholars believe that before the land on which the temple will be built can be purified, these ashes must be discovered and applied.

In Ezekiel 36:24-25 the Lord promises that He will take the Jewish people out of the nations and that He will sprinkle clean water on them and they will be clean. At present there is a serious archaeological dig in progress, based on solid evidence derived from scrolls found at Qumran, located on the shores of the Dead Sea. If such a discovery were to be made, this could be the spark that sets in motion a great resurgence of interest among Jews of their rich heritage.

The other aspect of this issue is this: Could there be some guarantee that any ashes found would contain original fragments of a red heifer from the days of Moses? Furthermore, the whole question of a great archaeological find almost becomes a non-event in the light of the fact that Israel has recently imported a shipment of pure breed red heifers from the United States. Therefore, if ashes of a red heifer are required for ceremonial cleansing, it would be a simple matter of producing them on demand.

Quite apart from this interesting item of Jewish history, the only temple that should interest God's people is the residence or the temple of His Holy Spirit, and that is our bodies. His Spirit dwells within each of us. We must protect and honour that dwelling place continually.

The Jewish temple was a physical building which was filled by God's *Shekinah* glory when the people were in fellowship with Jehovah. The future Tribulation (third) temple will be the place where the Jews will initially reintroduce the sacrificial system but it will be done without the blessing of Jehovah.[28]

When Jesus Christ physically reigns from Mount Zion in Jerusalem, only memorial sacrifices in the millennial temple will be performed, and will receive the blessing of the King of kings and Lord of lords (Zech. 14:16).

77. Question: How important is the Temple Mount in Bible prophecy?

Answer: Psalm 132:13-14 was written by King David, the man responsible for initiating plans to build the first permanent Jewish temple on Mount Moriah. This particular passage sums up so succinctly the importance of the Temple Mount in Bible prophecy:

> For the Lord has chosen Zion, he has desired it for his dwelling: "This is my resting place for ever and ever; here I will sit enthroned, for I have desired it."

There is no greater thrill for the Christian pilgrim on his

or her maiden journey to the Holy Land than the first glimpse of the old city of Jerusalem from the Mount of Olives. There, central to the whole panorama, is the magnificent Muslim structure of the "Dome of the Rock" standing resplendent atop of the holy mountain — Mount Moriah.

However, compared to the world's more grander mountains, this mount hardly seems worthy of the name. It is, in physical terms, little more than a hill. Nonetheless, this hill, according to God's Word, is the place on earth, the place in Israel, the place in Jerusalem, where the Lord God chose to make His name abide forever.

As the heart of the land of Israel is Jerusalem, so the heart of Jerusalem is the Temple Mount. When Solomon dedicated his magnificent temple to God, he declared in 2 Chronicles 6:10: "I have built the temple for the Name of the Lord, the God of Israel."

Over the years the Jewish temples have been a reminder that it has always been God's desire to dwell among His people. The glory of God (*Shekinah*) was present in Solomon's Temple in the form of a cloud resident in the Holy of Holies. The glory of God in the personage of God's Son Jesus Christ spent much time in Herod's Temple. But there has been no more painful and tragic day of memories for Israel than *Tisha B'Av*. For it was on the ninth day of July, first in 586 B.C. and again in A.D. 70, that both temples located on Mount Moriah were destroyed.

Since 1967, when Israel gained control of Jerusalem, it has been the heart-filled desire of every Orthodox Jew to prepare for the rebuilding of the temple. Many within the ranks of Judaism view rebuilding the temple as a precursor to the coming of the Messiah. They believe that only when the temple stands again on Mount Moriah, will their Messiah come.

As Christians, we know from the prophetic Word that a temple will be rebuilt somewhere on the Temple Mount, and that it must be rebuilt by the middle of the Tribulation

(Dan. 9:27). How this can be possible given the current political situation together with a strong Muslim presence and their claim to the Temple Mount as the third most holy site for Islam, only God knows.

The Word of God does, however, confirm that the Lord will return and choose Jerusalem as His dwelling place and rebuild His temple as a place of worship for all peoples and nations:

> "Therefore, this is what the Lord says: 'I will return to Jerusalem with mercy, and there my house will be rebuilt. And the measuring line will be stretched out over Jerusalem,' declares the Lord Almighty. Proclaim further: This is what the Lord Almighty says: 'My towns will again overflow with prosperity, and the Lord will again comfort Zion and choose Jerusalem' " (Zech. 1:16-17).

Only when this is accomplished, and when Israel has been restored in her relationship to God, will true and lasting peace come to the Middle East and the whole world. This will happen as the Bible foreshadows during the Millennium, the thousand-year reign of Jesus Christ on planet Earth.

What will it be like on the Temple Mount during this period of peace and prosperity?

The prophet Micah tells it all:

> In the last days the mountain of the Lord's temple will be established as chief among the mountains; it will be raised above the hills, and peoples will stream to it. Many nations will come and say, "Come, let us go up to the mountain of the Lord, to the house of the God of Jacob. He will teach us his ways, so that we may walk in his paths." The law will go out from Zion, the word of the Lord from Jerusalem. He will judge between

many peoples and will settle disputes for strong nations far and wide. They will beat their swords into plowshares and their spears into pruning hooks. Nation will not take up sword against nation, nor will they train for war any more (Mic. 4:1-3).

The Glorious Hope for the Christian

The Bulletin of Atomic Scientists has for many years pictured a clock on its cover. The positions of its hands show the time as minutes before midnight. According to this symbolism, when both hands reach midnight, humankind will have brought about its own demise. The question that people across the globe are asking is, "What does the future hold?" "Will there be a tomorrow?"

Knowing that the present world order would not last forever, the apostle Peter asked a significant question: "Since everything will be destroyed in this way [by fire], what kind of people ought you to be? You ought to live holy and godly lives as you look forward to the day of God and speed its coming" (2 Pet. 3:11-12).

One of Peter's objects in writing his two epistles was to emphasize the **hope** for the believer of the Lord's return. He anticipates the scoffer's challenge, " 'Where is this "coming" he promised?' " (2 Pet. 3:4) by showing that Christ's second coming has been foretold by the prophets; and foreshadowed from creation, the Flood, the corridors of time, and God's mercy (2 Pet. 3:1-2,4,6,8-9).

The world may scoff at the Christian's belief in the Lord's imminent return. In Peter's day scoffers looked at the world around them and could detect no outward change. They were certain in their own minds that the belief that Christ would return and that the world would end had no substance.

Two thousand years later nothing has changed. The world today has chosen to ignore the clear signs of Christ's return in power and great glory, which will ultimately result in the destruction of this world.

To scoff at the belief in the second coming of Christ is to ignore one historical fact: God destroyed the world once before.

Believing Christians have never centered their lives in this world alone. We have always known that we are citizens of two worlds. While the end of the world carries a threat of judgment and destruction, it also carries a blessed hope. We know that God has prepared a greater world in which to live. It will be an eternal world which knows no end. This world is not our home; heaven is our eternal home.

The promise of Christ's coming should have an immediate practical affect upon our lives. It should make us increasingly holy, godly, and busy. Holiness should always be our aim. Scripture clearly exhorts us to live wholesome Christian lives in anticipation of Christ's coming. This is not the time for that one last fling or for sowing wild oats while we can. If anything, today's climate is an incentive for a deeper Christian experience and witness.

In more than one place in this chapter (2 Pet. 3:9,15) we are told that the delay of Christ's return is for our own good. It gives us an opportunity to witness and an opportunity for the lost to accept salvation.

Christ is coming. That's our ultimate hope. Our immediate hope is to ensure that when He does come we may be "found spotless, blameless and at peace with him" (2 Pet. 3:14).

Notes

[1] Ray Yerbury, *The Ultimate Event — A Bible Study in Prophecy* (Brisbane, Australia: Cross Publications, 1988), p. 7-12.

[2] Yerbury, *The Ultimate Event—A Bible Study in Prophecy*, p. 1-6.

[3] A.R. Fausset, *Bible Encyclopedia and Dictionary — Critical & Expository* (Grand Rapids, MI: Zondervan Publishing House), p. 471.

[4] *The Illustrated Bible Dictionary* (Leicester, Great Britain: Inter-Varsity Press, 1980), page 1535.

[5] *Your Tomorrow,* Volume 3, number 3, June 1989, page 7.

[6] C.I. Scofield, Scofield Bible Correspondance Course (Chicago, IL: Moody Bible Institute, 1907), vol. 3.

[7] *World Book Encyclopedia* (Chicago, IL: Field Enterprises Corporation, 1974), vol. 10, page 390.

[8] John Knox, *The History of the Reformation of Religion Within the Realm of Scotland* (Edinburgh: The Banner of Truth Trust, 1982).

[9] *Your Tomorrow,* vol. 1, no. 10, January 1988, page 3.

[10] F. John Walvoord, *Daniel, the Key to Prophetic Revelation* (Chicago, IL: Moody Press, 1971).

[11] Walter Scott, *Exposition of the Revelation of Jesus Christ* (Longdon, England: Pickering & Inglis, Ltd.)

[12] Yerbury, *The Ultimate Event,* pages 156-159.

[13] *Midnight Call,* May 1984, page 17.

[14] *Midnight Call,* September 1988, page 17.

[15] Scot Overbey, *Vladimir Ahirinovsky — The Man Who Would Be Gog* (Oklahoma City, OK: Hearthstone Publishing, Ltd., 1994), page 122.

[16] Don Stanton, *Maranatha Prophetic Alert,* News report no. 47, article from Reuter News Correspondant, Secunderabad, India, 5/31/89.

[17] *Asia Week,* 5/19/89.

[18] *Midnight Call,* May 1988, page 18.

[19] Texe Marrs, *Dark Secrets of the New Age* (Westchester, IL: Crossway Books, 1987).

[20] S. Marshall, *The Crystal Calling* (Sydney, N.S.W., Australia: Aurora Press, 1986).

[21] *Prophetic Alert,* no. 50, June 1989, page 14.

[22] *The Courier Mail, Qld,* Australia, 9/21/89, page 5.

[23] *The Courier Mail,* Qld, Australia, 1/23/89, page 7.

[24] *Midnight Call,* September 1985, page 20.

[25] Thomas Ice, "What Is Dominion Theology?" *Biblical Perspective,* vol. 1, no. 3, May/June 1988.

[26] *The Sunday Mail, Qld.,* Australia, "Wildlife Album-II," page 38-39.

[27] *Your Tomorrow,* vol. 3, no. 3, June 1989, page 3.

[28] International Christian Assembly, Jerusalem, June 1989.

[29] *Time* magazine, 10/16/89, page 80-81.

Bibliography

Anderson, Robert. *The Coming Prince.* London: Hodder & Stoughton, Reprinted 1985.

Chacour, Elais. *Blood Brothers.* Sussex, Great Britain: Kingsway Publications Ltd, 1986.

Chapman, Colin. *Whose Promised Land?* London: Lion Publishing Company, 1983.

Clouse, G. Robert. *The Meaning of the Millennium — Four Views.* Wheaton, IL: Inter Varsity Press, 1977.

Davis & Whitcomb. *A History of Israel.* Grand Rapids, MI: Baker Book House, 1980.

Douglas & Tenney. *The New International Dictionary of the Bible.* Hants,UK: Marshall Pickering Publishers, 1987.

Fausset, A.R. *Bible Encyclopedia and Dictionary* — Critical & Expository. Grand Rapids, MI: Zondervan, undated.

Friederichsen, Paul. *Prophecy Unveiled — Revelation Simplified.* Brisbane, Australia. Evangelistic Literature Ent, 1989.

Geisler, Norman. *A Popular Survey of the Old Testament.* Grand Rapids, MI: Baker Book House, 1977.

Halley, H. Henry. *Halley's Bible Handbook.* Grand Rapids, MI: Zondervan Publishing House, 24th Ed., 1965.

The Illustrated Bible Dictionary. Parts 1,2,3. Leicester, G.B: Inter-Varsity Press, 1980.

Ironside, H.A. *Lectures on Daniel the Prophet.* New York: Loizeaux Brothers, 1986.

Keil,C.F. & Delitzsch, F. *Commentary on the Old Testament.* Grand Rapids, MI: W.B. Eerdmans Publishing, 1951.

Knox, John. *The History of the Reformation of Religion Within the Realm of Scotland.* Edinburgh: The Banner of Truth Trust, 1982.

LaHaye, Tim. *The Beginning of the End.* Wheaton, IL: Tyndale House Publishers, 1981.

LaHaye, Tim. *Life in the Afterlife,* Wheaton, IL: Tyndale, 1980.

LaHaye,Tim. *Revelation.* Grand Rapids, MI: Zondervan, 1979.

Lindsey, Hal. *There's A New World Coming.* Santa Ana, CA. Harvest House Publishers, 1973.

Lindsey, Hal, *The Late Great Planet Earth.* Melbourne, Australia: S.John Bacon, 1970.

The Lion Handbook to the Bible. Herts, G.B: Lion Pub. 1981.

Ludwigson, R. *A Survey of Bible Prophecy.* Grand Rapids, MI: Zondervan Publishing Corp., 1975.

Marrs, Texe. *Dark Secrets of the New Age.* Westchester, IL: Crossway Books, 1987.

Mc Farland & Kincheloe. *A Personal Adventure in Prophecy.* Wheaton IL. Tyndale House Publishers, 1974.

Midnight Call Magazine. West Columbia, SC: Midnight Call Inc. 1985-1989.

New Bible Dictionary, 2nd. Ed. Wheaton, IL: Tyndale House, 1982.

Packer, Merrill, Tenney, White. *All the People and Places of the Bible.* Nashville, TN: Thomas Nelson, Inc., 1982.

Payne, J. Barton. *Encyclopedia of Bible Prophecy.* Grand Rapids, MI: Baker Book House, 1973.

Pentecost, J. Dwight. *Things to come.* Grand Rapids, MI: Zondervan Publishing House, 1958.

Scofield, C.I. *Scofield Bible Correspondance Course.* Vol.3. Chicago, IL: Moody Bible Institute, 1907.

Scott, Walter. *Exposition of the Revelation of Jesus Christ.* London: Pickering & Inglis Ltd. 4th Ed. undated.

Stanton. E. Don. *Mystery 666.* Perth, Australia: Maranatha Revival Crusade, 11th ed., 1988.

Stanton, E. Don. *Maranatha Prophetic Alert News Reports.* Secunderabad, India. 1988-1994.

Unger, F. Merrill. *The New Unger's Bible Handbook.* Chicago, IL: Moody Press, 1984.

Walvoord, F. John. *Daniel, the Key to Prophetic Revelation.* Chicago, Illinois: Moody Press, 1971.

Walvoord, F. John. *The Revelation of Jesus Christ:* A Commentary. Chicago, IL: Moody Press,1966.

Willmington, H.L. *The King is Coming.* Wheaton, IL: Tyndale House Publishers, 1983.

Wood, Leon. *A Commentary on Daniel.* Grand rapids, MI: Zondervan Publishing House, 1973.

The World Book Encyclopedia. USA: Field Enterprises Corporation, 1974.

Your Tomorrow Publication. Sussex, G.B: Prophetic Witness Publishing House.

Yerbury, Ray W. *God's Blueprint for Planet Earth.* Brisbane, Australia: Cross Publications, 1992.

Yerbury, Ray W. *Prophecies of Daniel.* Brisbane, Australia: Cross Publications, 1988.

Yerbury, Ray W. *The Ultimate Event - A Bible Study in Prophecy.* Brisbane, Australia: Cross Publications, 1988.